Leadership Accelerated

WORKBOOK

Own Your Growth. Shape Your Path.
Lead Your Way.

Angie McDermott, PhD

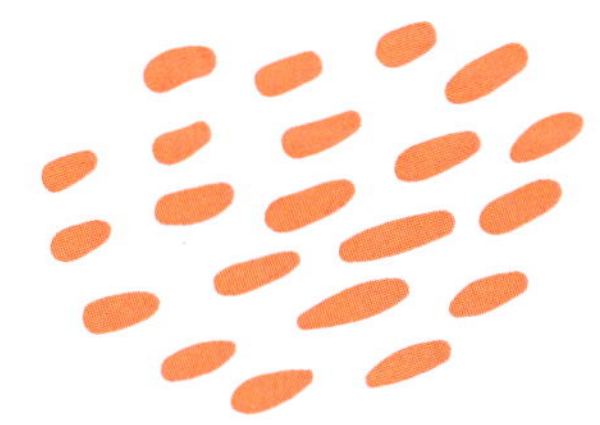

Dedicated to Max, Mackenzie, Annie, Kate,
and my wonderful students and clients

ISBN: 979-8-9933624-0-3
Printed in the United States of America
Designed and Packaged by Weller Smith Design

10 9 8 7 6 5 4 3 2 1
First Edition
Published by McDermott Group Consulting, LLC

This workbook belongs to:

Table of Contents

"If you're always trying to be normal, you will never know how amazing you can be."

–**Maya Angelou** (poet, author, civil rights activist, voice of resilience and empowerment)

Dear Reader,

The world needs you. The world needs you to step up and fulfill your leadership potential.

My plea is urgent, given that so many of our leaders seem to have lost their way, while waves of change and challenges keep hitting our world at an impossibly accelerated rate. The climate emergency, rising global nationalism, the threat of other pandemics, and devastating wars, to name a few, continue to polarize our country, potentially impacting your businesses and our way of life. Don't expect the waves of change to stop coming. It's both a truism and our reality that change is our only constant.

Your leadership dramatically impacts the people who follow you, the clients you serve, and the communities in which you live. We desperately need you to grow into your potential and make it your business to bring other leaders along with you on this journey. It's an exciting time to be part of a movement of leaders who bravely show up as they are in workplaces evolving to more inclusive environments, genuinely trying to tap into everyone's potential. In the face of ongoing societal challenges, it's disheartening to see efforts toward inclusion and diversity being questioned or even undone in many circles. As leaders, we must not only protect the progress we've made but continue to champion environments where everyone's potential is fully realized.

I've witnessed remarkable transformations throughout my career. My first job out of graduate school was with a global consumer products company that had been around for more than 100 years. Their stories

"The most effective way to do it, is to do it."

–Amelia Earhart (aviator, pioneer, advocate for women's rights, record-breaking explorer)

could take you back to the Civil War era. At the time, the leadership was made up entirely of white men, working in offices with wood paneling and dark portraits of former leaders lining the halls. Early in my career, I felt I had to be very "buttoned up" and near perfect. I often felt inauthentic–an impostor in my navy suit with a bow tie. Fast forward to my last corporate role, where leaders sat alongside their teams, and jeans and T-shirts became the norm. The old power structures are shifting, and new models of leadership are emerging. Despite the challenges, there has never been a better time for you to step up and lead–regardless of gender, race, sexual orientation, neurodiversity, or other differences that once might hold you back from a brilliant career.

This process works best if you are currently in the workplace with at least two years of experience. It also works for people in their mid- to late-career stage who are motivated to keep learning and achieving.

Now, at the tail end of my career, I'm focused on helping leaders accelerate their development. We don't have time to let you grow casually or without intention. We need more than a handful of leaders selected for your company's exclusive leadership development program. If you want to fulfill your potential as a leader, it's time to get focused and deliberate. This workbook empowers you to take control of your development to help you achieve great things beyond your wildest dreams and tackle the challenges life throws your way.

Angie McDermott

How to Use This Workbook

This workbook is designed to adapt to your needs, so use the most natural and effective approach for you. Choose your own adventure!

Follow the workbook step by step: Dive in from start to finish, answering reflective questions and completing the exercises as you go. When you're done, fill out the What Matters Most and Development Plan for Leaders templates. Treat these as living documents that evolve with your career—your roadmap to success.

Focus on your priorities: Jump straight to the sections that your assessment (at the end of Chapter 1) highlights as key opportunities. Start there to uncover impactful ways to kick-start or accelerate your leadership growth. Once you've tackled those areas, circle back to explore the rest of the workbook.

Collaborate with a trusted circle: Team up with a small group of trusted friends or colleagues. Work through the exercises together, and after each chapter, share your insights. Their perspectives might just unlock new dimensions of your leadership journey.

A tool for executive coaches: Use this guide with your clients to create a robust plan that accelerates their development.

No matter the path you choose, this workbook is here to empower you. I know you are ready to do the work. Let's get you to your rightful place. This is your time to shine!

So, let's begin.

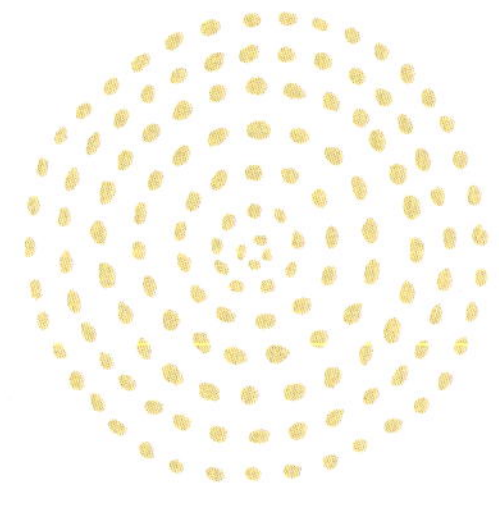

Acknowledgements

As I share my approach with you, know that I'm standing on the shoulders of some extraordinary researchers who spent their careers trying to understand how leaders develop. I draw heavily on the thoughtful work of researchers and corporate collaborators associated with the Center of Creative Leadership—the book that shaped so many in my field was *The Lessons of Experience: How Successful Executives Develop on the Job* by Morgan McCall, Michael Lombardo, and Ann Morrison, published way back in 1988.[1] Later, Michael Lombardo and Bob Eichinger and others continued their work building a consulting practice (Lominger) and providing research and tools for people like myself. I reference their summary work, *The Leadership Machine*,[2] throughout. Lastly, I draw upon the work of Ken De Meuse and Veronica Schmidt Harvey, who collaborated with academics and practitioners to bring us the *Age of Agility*.[3] I am grateful and humbled by all their contributions to helping leaders grow into their potential.

It truly took a village—both personally and professionally—to bring this workbook to life.

Charissa Samaniego, PhD, played a critical role in refining and validating the Accelerator assessment, offering invaluable support and feedback on earlier drafts. The insightful input of Mackenzie Krys on the later drafts pushed me to challenge my ideas in the best possible way.

The incredible team at Weller Smith Design LLC—LeAnna Smith and Erin Williams—became my workbook whisperers, guiding me through the design process with expertise and care. I couldn't have done it without them.

A warm thanks to all my "believing mirrors" cheering me on every step of the way—especially Kathleen Woodhouse and Margaret Keys.

And finally, Paul Strelzick's consistent encouragement, love, and support helped make all this possible.

Thank you all for your unwavering belief in me and this project.

"Define success on your own terms, achieve it by your own rules, and build a life you're proud to live."

–**ANNE SWEENEY** (former president of Walt Disney/ ABC Television)[4]

SETTING THE STAGE: THE FRAMEWORK, BASIC ASSUMPTIONS, AND A QUICK DIAGNOSTIC

Setting the Stage: The Framework, Basic Assumptions, and a Quick Diagnostic

In this chapter, you'll discover a framework to fast-track your growth and unlock your leadership potential.

We'll dive into the key assumptions that form the foundation of this work and kick-start a transformative process to reshape how you grow as a leader. Get ready to challenge old habits, embrace new insights, and take actionable steps toward becoming the leader you aspire to be.

By the end of this chapter, you'll have your results from a quick assessment that will identify your most significant opportunities to boost your development as a leader.

Imagine for a moment that we're sitting across from one another with a fresh cup of coffee.

I would start by asking you more about yourself—successes, obstacles, joys, and dreams. I already know you want something more. You might be frustrated or feel stuck in your job without a clear path forward. You may want more power, recognition, and impact on the world around you.

As I learn more about you, I'll remind you that leaders are made, not born. ***Leadership is learned.*** You have what it takes to become an impactful leader without showing up as someone you are not. I'll encourage you to discover how to thrive as a leader by tapping into your strengths, experiences, and motivation. I'll also remind you that you are not alone on this journey. Many support you and your growth.

I've had the privilege of working with hundreds of courageous leaders throughout my career. The most enlightened leaders I know make their development a conscious process and a way of life for themselves and those they lead. If this is what you seek, we'll make an excellent team. I hope you feel my supportive presence as you embrace this work.

In this workbook, I'll provide you with a leadership development framework designed to accelerate your growth by focusing on your strengths and embracing what makes you unique, rather than simply fixing weaknesses or molding you to fit someone else's idea of effective leadership. There's both a science and an art to your growth. Rest assured, both are embedded in the pages that follow. Get ready to unlock your potential and lead with confidence and purpose.

Leadership Development for Everyone

In many larger companies, high-impact leadership programs are thoughtfully designed—but only for a select few. Most of us, however, work in organizations without the luxury of dedicated leadership development professionals. And even in companies with exceptional programs, access is often limited. One executive recently shared that out of 1,000 people in his organization, he could nominate only three for a leadership development program.

What about everyone else? That's where this workbook comes in. I have designed it for *all* leaders who are worried about their ongoing development and the development of the people around them.

The Accelerator Framework

There are four key elements you can use to accelerate your development. Knowing your current development approach pinpoints the most significant opportunities for fast-tracking your growth. Master accelerating your development, and you'll reach (or at least get closer) to your unknowable potential, with or without your company's support and funding. In the chapters ahead, we'll dive deeper into each element.

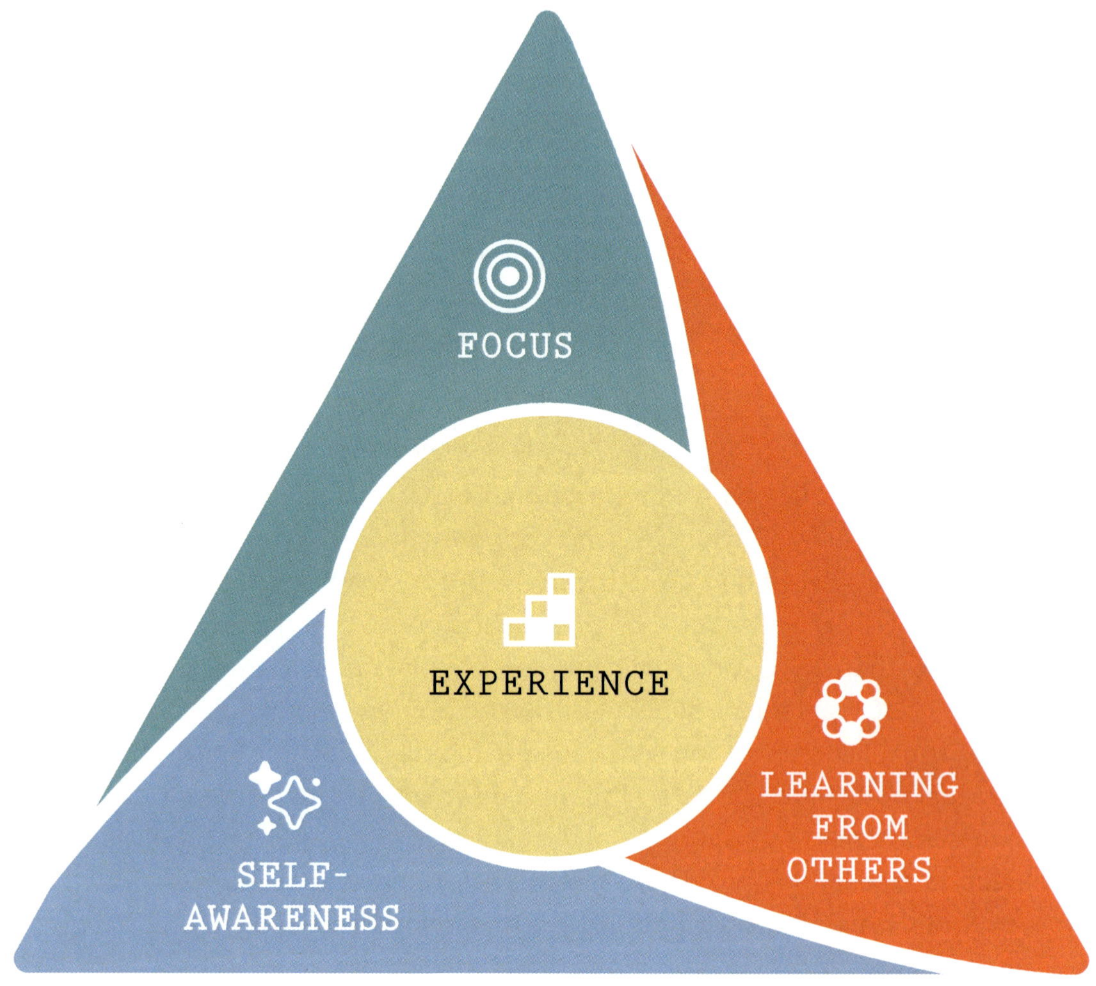

NERD ALERT:

This framework evolved from the widely used 70-20-10 framework (although, let's be honest, its origins remain a bit of a mystery[5]). The original framework suggests that seventy percent of leadership development comes from the hard-earned lessons of direct experience, twenty percent from learning through others, and ten percent from formal training programs or courses. While the foundation of this framework remains central, I've taken the liberty to adapt, refine, and add to it. One thing remains constant: real-world experience is still the cornerstone of your growth. But, I get ahead of myself.

Increasing self-awareness

Self-awareness is foundational to effective leadership. Highly self-aware leaders are more confident, make sounder decisions, get more promotions, and are more effective leaders overall.[6] We'll spend a great deal of time and energy here because it dramatically influences the goals you set, your engagement with others, and how you maximize your learning through experiences.

Self-Awareness[7] involves two dimensions:

1. **What Matters Most:** Your primary roles, values, strengths, vulnerabilities, and true desires.
2. **Understanding How Others Experience You:** How your actions and behaviors impact others.

On a scale from 1-10 (with 10 being the best), how clear are you on what matters most to you? How well do you know how others perceive your leadership?

In Chapter 2, we'll dive deeper into your self-awareness. We'll help you articulate what's important to you (roles, values, etc.) and how others view your leadership.

Harnessing the power of focus

Focus is about having clear goals and aligning your actions with your long-term aspirations. It helps you direct your energy and allows others to support you.

How clear are your short and long-term personal and professional goals? Are your goals known to others?

In Chapter 3, we'll help you clarify your goals and ensure they align with your values. We'll encourage you to share them with those around you—your manager, your mentor, or trusted peers.

Leveraging work (and life) experiences

Work and life experiences are the most powerful tools for growth. By actively engaging with the challenges in your current role and stepping out of your comfort zone, you can drastically accelerate your leadership development. To enhance your lessons learned, augment your experience by adding the habit of reflection.

To what extent are you learning on the job or being pushed outside your comfort zone? How often do you reflect on your experiences?

In Chapter 4, we'll give you ideas on how to better leverage your job to accelerate your development and challenge you to actively seek new opportunities that stretch your abilities.

Learning from others

Leadership growth doesn't happen in isolation. It is a team sport and requires learning from others through direct mentoring, observing successful leaders, or engaging with a supportive network. This is especially important if you depend on the decisions of others to place you in new assignments and/or to get promoted. How well are you tapping into the wisdom of other successful, influential leaders?

In Chapter 5, we'll help you identify the people who can significantly influence your leadership progress and development.

These four key elements work in a dynamic, interconnected way—each one enhancing and reinforcing the others. Experience is where the magic happens, but it can only take you so far if you're not clear about your direction (Focus), out of sync with your values and priorities (Self-Awareness), or disconnected from the wisdom and insights of others. Together, these elements create a powerful formula for accelerating your learning and leadership effectiveness.

Six Fundamental Assumptions for Leadership Development

Over the years of working with executives, I've uncovered a set of core assumptions that shape how I approach this work. Let's explore them together and see how they align with or enhance your current leadership development strategy.

You have one life

In this 24/7 world, personal and business lives overlap and, for many, collide. Gone are the simple days of 9-to-5. Keeping your work life and your personal life in nice, neat containers no longer applies when you're juggling that evening conference call while cooking dinner for several hungry people, while your partner is folding laundry and keeping the homework moving. We can't ignore your life goals outside your business life. This is our modern reality. But here's the truth: **Winning at work should not mean you are losing in the rest of your life.** Together, let's craft a strategy for your "one big juicy life," where your personal and professional aspirations align and flourish.

Take a deep breath and think honestly–how balanced is your life right now? If one side of the scale feels heavier, what steps can you take today to restore equilibrium? What's one thing you can do differently next week?

You own it

You own your career and your development plan. Period. Full stop. Waiting for your organization to map out your future? Don't count on it. Even if they have a plan (highly unlikely), you must be the driver of your own growth. Don't assume your manager knows how–or has the time, energy, or enthusiasm–to help you grow. Here's the hard truth: Most leaders are not great at developing others. In fact, they're downright terrible. According to Lombardo and Eichinger, the competency "Developing Others" ranks dead last–67th out of 67 competencies–across individual contributors, managers, and executives.[8] Let that sink in. Scary, isn't it? The good news? Taking charge of your development puts the power squarely in your hands.

Think about how your growth has been supported (or not supported) so far. How can you take charge and become your biggest advocate?

When you finish this workbook, you will have a personal development plan with clear steps to enhance your leadership capabilities. Look at you taking ownership of your growth!

Leverage your strengths to achieve success and supercharge your growth

Leadership isn't a one-size-fits-all approach—every leader brings their own unique set of talents to the table. By leaning into your strengths, success becomes not only more achievable but also more enjoyable. Your strengths are also powerful tools for growth. For example, if "strategic agility" is one of your top strengths and you're working on improving delegation, why not develop a strategy that makes delegation seamless and impactful? By aligning your strengths with your development goals, you can unlock your full leadership potential. Let's identify what makes you exceptional and use it to fuel your success and growth journey.

Think of a time recently when you really felt like you were in your element at work. What strengths were at play? How can you leverage more of these strengths to increase your impact?

In Chapter 2, we'll help you identify your strengths and reflect on how they

contribute to your leadership success. Look for opportunities to leverage these strengths in your current role and beyond. Consider how you can further amplify them to achieve your leadership goals.

Leadership development is personal development

Leadership development is a bold, transformative journey—not for the faint of heart. It requires the courage to reflect deeply on what truly matters in your life, to confront your strengths and limitations, and to evaluate whether your current path aligns with your personal and professional goals. The commitment to ongoing. Rapid growth can be humbling. You'll face moments that challenge your ego in the best possible way. And the payoff? A profound "aha moment" that shifts your perspective, ignites your inner potential, and leaves you inspired to lead with renewed clarity and purpose.

To what extent are you ready to start this journey? Who can you turn to when you may need another's perspective or some encouragement? Think about one or two people who can offer support, feedback, and guidance. This could be people like your manager, mentor, peer, or coach.

Are you ready to commit to the leadership development journey ahead? Reach out and begin a conversation about your growth with the people you listed to ensure you have a support system in place. More on this in Chapter 5.

What got you here won't get you there[9]

Every new leadership level you achieve will demand new ways of thinking and a different set of skills. Being a whiz at digging into the details as an individual contributor might have gotten you noticed, but if you overuse that superpower as you become a higher-level leader, it may stifle your progress. Your new role may demand a more strategic view of the business, and focusing too much on the details will lead you to miss the big picture or not see the volatile changes charging at you and your organization. Lifelong, agile learning isn't just a nice-to-have—it's your compass for long-term success and, quite honestly, your edge for survival in an ever-changing world.

What might you need to unlearn as you progress to the next level? What might you need to learn?

Reflect on the habits, behaviors, or mindsets that might be holding you back. What old ways of thinking or doing things might you need to leave behind? On the flip side, identify new skills or mindsets you need to develop. Set clear actions for what you need to unlearn and learn to grow as a leader.

Leadership development is a life-long journey

Leadership isn't a destination—it's an ongoing adventure filled with twists, turns, and unexpected detours. Along the way, you'll celebrate wins, but you'll also face setbacks and hit roadblocks. It's inevitable. This journey is a way of life, one that spans your entire career—and ideally, beyond. The key is to view every misstep as a learning opportunity. When you stumble (and you will), pick yourself up, uncover the leadership lesson hidden in the challenge, and keep moving forward. Celebrate the small victories, embrace the tough moments, and remember that each step shapes the leader you are becoming.

Visualize the trajectory of your career and the legacy you want to leave. Sketch out your journey, both the past and future, and think about the pivotal moments and decisions that will shape your leadership path. Set intentional goals for where you want to be in the coming years and ensure your actions align with that vision.

Take the Assessment

Before moving on to the next chapter, take a moment to complete the Accelerator–A Development Diagnostic. This assessment can help pinpoint your most significant opportunities to supercharge your development. It will take about three minutes to complete and will provide you with your results and some suggestions right after you complete it. Imagine clearly understanding where you stand and what steps will propel you forward.

REFLECTION

WRITE YOUR RESULTS FROM THE ACCELERATOR BELOW.

	Score	Rating			
Overall		o High	o Moderately High	o Moderately Low	o Low
Self-Awareness		o High	o Moderately High	o Moderately Low	o Low
Focus		o High	o Moderately High	o Moderately Low	o Low
Experience		o High	o Moderately High	o Moderately Low	o Low
Learning from Others		o High	o Moderately High	o Moderately Low	o Low

WHAT SUGGESTIONS LISTED IN THE REPORT MAKE SENSE TO YOU AT THIS POINT? ANY SURPRISES?

BASED ON THIS ASSESSMENT, WHAT'S THE ONE THING YOU COULD DO TO BOOST YOUR DEVELOPMENT AS A LEADER?

Wrap-Up and Next Steps

In this chapter, we introduced a framework designed to fast-track your development and completed an assessment to super-boost your growth as a leader.

Next, we'll explore self-awareness in four focused sections. There's a lot to unpack, so tackle each section at your own pace and take breaks to reflect and recharge.

“Self-awareness is the key to wellness, to energy, to a fulfilling life, and to better leadership.”

–ARIANNA HUFFINGTON

(author; publisher and co-founder of HuffPost; founder and CEO of Thrive Global)

2

INCREASING SELF-AWARENESS

Increasing Self-Awareness

In this chapter, you'll start enhancing your self-awareness. There's a lot to cover, so I've broken it into four sections. Work through each section, giving yourself some time to reflect between each.

1. What Is Self-Awareness, and Why Is It Important?
Discover the two primary dimensions of self-awareness and the benefits of enhancing it.

2. Internal Self-Awareness: What Matters Most
Explore what values guide you, your strengths that differentiate you, and your vulnerabilities to navigate. Draft your purpose statement and leadership narrative.

3. External Self-Awareness: How Others Experience You
Learn why it's critical to know how others perceive you and the methods you can use to get feedback. Do some field work.

4. Growth Mindset: Enhancing Your Approach to Change
Discover why having a growth mindset matters to your progress.

By the end of this chapter, you will have a draft of What Matters Most to you.

> *"It takes courage to grow up and become who you really are."*
>
> –**E. E. Cummings** (a groundbreaking poet who defied conventional form and structure)

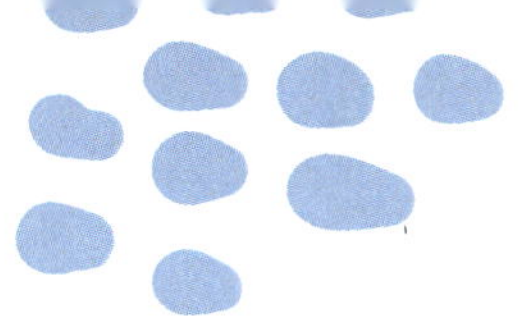

1. What Is Self-Awareness, and Why Is It Important?

Let me start this section on self-awareness with a confession. Early in my coaching days, as I approached how to help my clients be better leaders, I followed the typical method of focusing on their weaknesses and vulnerabilities. These flat spots usually showed up as the lowest scores on a 360 assessment or as negative feedback from their boss or peers. I took the same approach in terms of my development as well.

What I learned over the years is that development plans focused on weaknesses felt lacking in energy and rarely created breakthroughs for my clients (or myself, for that matter). After crafting a thoughtful plan, clients would simply not do the work to make it happen. What was missing was the hook to something uplifting and motivating—the big "why" or the strong alignment with what people value. So, for example, in the client story on page 26, Self-Awareness in Action, if we had focused solely on Helen's vulnerability (controlling her emotions), she may not have experienced a breakthrough in her career.

It became apparent that the upfront work on getting clear on personal values and strengths, and declaring professional goals, set my clients on a path to a much more powerful, accelerated development plan.

So, before we start figuring out your accelerated development plan, let's take stock of what's important to you. Enhancing your self-awareness is "inside-out work." Organizational researcher and executive coach Tasha Eurich, in her 2017 book *Insight: Why We're Not as Self-Aware as We Think, and How Seeing Ourselves Clearly Helps Us Succeed at Work and in Life,*[13] lays out a two-by-two model that resonates with how I think of this work. The first dimension is knowing what you value and stand for, and entails

NERD ALERT:

It turns out researchers have a name for this self-directed approach—protean career orientation.[10] Douglas Hall suggested that when we "pursue a path with heart with the intensity of a calling," our work becomes filled with personal meaning. He defined this approach as "a career that is self-determined, driven by personal values rather than organizational rewards, and serving the whole person, family, and life purpose." And there's plenty of evidence that having this orientation to our career leads to many positive outcomes we all hope for, like higher career satisfaction[11] and better work/life balance.[12]

SELF-AWARENESS IN ACTION

Helen, a long-time client and technology leader, reached out after being fired. As we unpacked what happened, she shared that she had publicly lost her cool with her boss. Helen had let her frustration with her boss's slow decision-making, indirectness, and unhealthy corporate politics build up to a boiling point. When I asked what she thought she learned from the situation, she told me, "While I know I need to better control my reactions, I also know I can no longer work for leaders I don't respect." It was difficult for her to stay even and composed when there was a dysfunctional void of leadership.

We then shifted to naming her strengths and vulnerabilities. She knew she needed a work situation that valued her bold leadership style, straight-shooting directness, and decisive decision-making. "My kryptonite is working with ineffective leaders who are not interested in others' perspectives." she said. "I'm ready to take a lead role as a CEO and pull together a great team that can have healthy debates and work together as a united front." Helen wanted to build an organization with a respectful yet fun culture. Once she clarified what had gone wrong and her strengths, vulnerabilities, and the kind of environment she thrived in, her insights about herself put her on a different path. She went on to lead several very successful companies as CEO. Helen used this moment of truth and set back to dig deeper, enhance her self-awareness, and set a new course for her career.

going inward and reflecting on what you really want. It's about getting very clear about the roles you serve and the values you hold dear. Cultivating your self-awareness is like discovering your inner compass or North Star.

The second dimension of this self-awareness journey involves understanding how others experience working with you. It's the external lens of the awareness puzzle. The goal is to discover gaps where people experience you differently than you perceive yourself. For example, you might think checking everyone's work is an act of being supportive, while others might perceive it as micromanaging or disempowering them. These gaps may be preventing you from having the impact you hope for or, at minimum, hinder your effectiveness. Knowing the positive ways you impact others and contribute to the greater good is also part of your exploration. You'll want to keep using and expanding these strengths. Seeking feedback from others exposes the good, the bad, and the ugly as we deepen our understanding of how we affect others. This clarity reinforces what you want and need to change, develop, or strengthen.

Take a look at the chart on the next page. The goal is to become an Aware leader possessing both high internal (what matters most to you) and external (how others see you) awareness while moving beyond being an Introspector, a Seeker, or a Pleaser.

The Four Self-Awareness Archetypes

(adapted from Tasha Eurich, 2017)

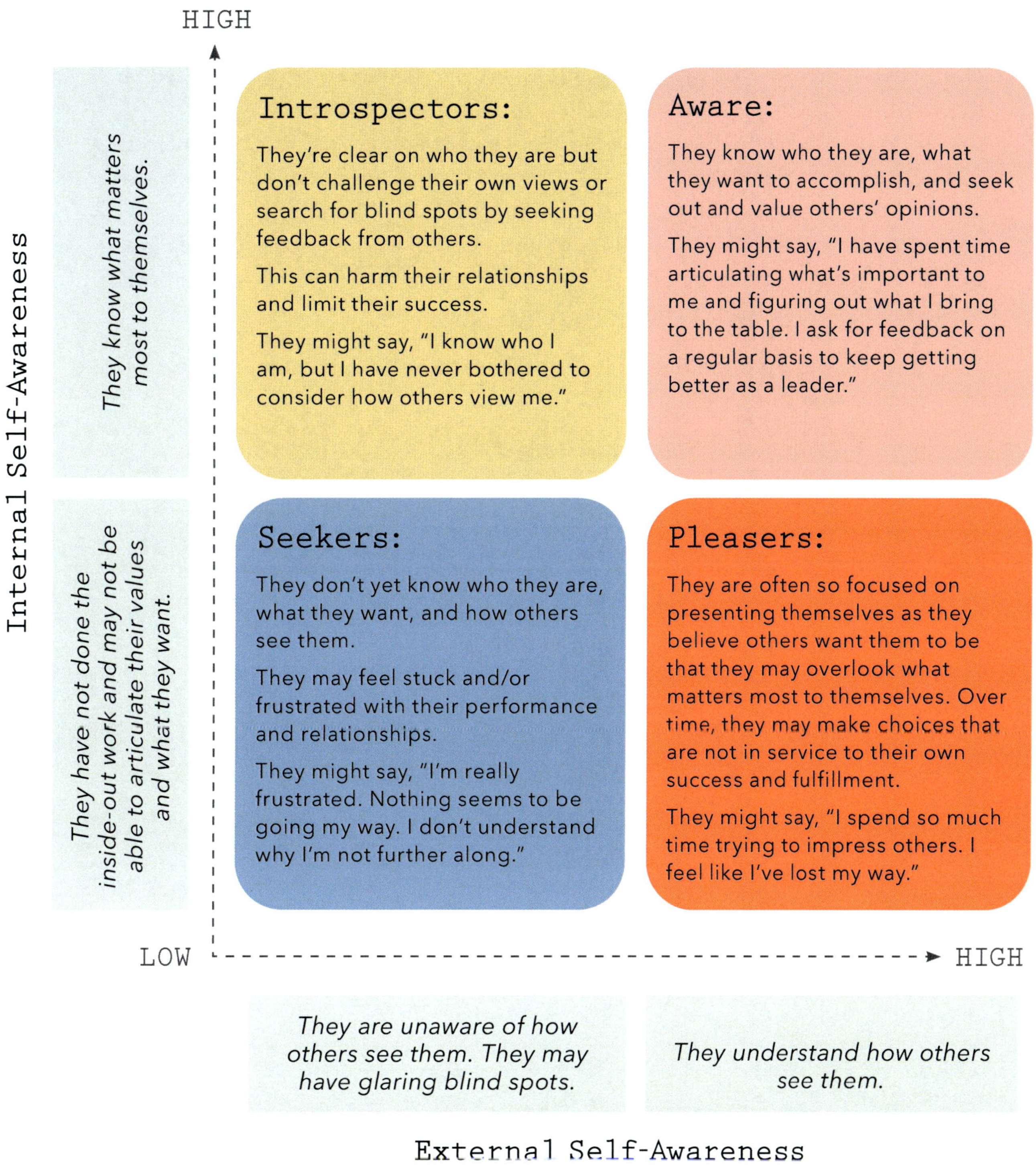

HIGH

Internal Self-Awareness

They know what matters most to themselves.

They have not done the inside-out work and may not be able to articulate their values and what they want.

Introspectors:

They're clear on who they are but don't challenge their own views or search for blind spots by seeking feedback from others.

This can harm their relationships and limit their success.

They might say, "I know who I am, but I have never bothered to consider how others view me."

Aware:

They know who they are, what they want to accomplish, and seek out and value others' opinions.

They might say, "I have spent time articulating what's important to me and figuring out what I bring to the table. I ask for feedback on a regular basis to keep getting better as a leader."

Seekers:

They don't yet know who they are, what they want, and how others see them.

They may feel stuck and/or frustrated with their performance and relationships.

They might say, "I'm really frustrated. Nothing seems to be going my way. I don't understand why I'm not further along."

Pleasers:

They are often so focused on presenting themselves as they believe others want them to be that they may overlook what matters most to themselves. Over time, they may make choices that are not in service to their own success and fulfillment.

They might say, "I spend so much time trying to impress others. I feel like I've lost my way."

LOW — HIGH

They are unaware of how others see them. They may have glaring blind spots.

They understand how others see them.

External Self-Awareness

At this point, you might be asking yourself, why bother going through a navel-gazing introspection followed by a feedback process that might be painful and uncomfortable?

Leaders with high self-awareness and a learning mindset are four times more effective in changing times.[14] Being self-aware also helps us adapt to shifting landscapes by adjusting our behavior to what's most appropriate and impactful in the moment. Our emotional intelligence—the ability to manage the emotions of others and, most notably, our feelings across a vast array of situations and encounters—grows as self-awareness increases.

The evidence is abundant: Increasing our self-awareness unlocks our potential. Researchers have demonstrated that self-aware leaders are better learners, have more confidence, are more creative, make sounder decisions, have stronger relationships, communicate more clearly, get more promotions, and are more effective leaders overall. It's a big piece of the Rosetta stone of creating the life you want. And self-awareness is easy for us to enhance. Just keep going.

You've just completed the first of four sections on Self-Awareness. Here's the road map for the next three sections:

Internal Awareness (What Matters Most)

1. Key Roles and Values
2. Purpose Statement and Leadership Narrative
3. Strengths and Vulnerabilities
4. Your Ideal Environment: Where Do You Thrive?

External Awareness (How Others See You)

1. Strengths and Vulnerabilities
2. Blind Spots

Growth Mindset: Enhancing Your Approach to Change

Keep going and complete this chapter. I believe in you!

REFLECTION

ARE YOU MORE INTERNALLY SELF-AWARE OR MORE EXTERNALLY SELF-AWARE? WHY DO YOU THINK THAT?

WHAT ARCHETYPE BEST DESCRIBES YOU AT THIS POINT? (INTROSPECTOR, AWARE, SEEKER, PLEASER) WHY DO YOU THINK THAT?

"Success is not the key to happiness. Happiness is the key to success. If you love what you are doing, you will be successful."

–Albert Schweitzer (humanitarian, philosopher, surgeon, Nobel Peace Prize laureate)

2. Internal Self-Awareness: What Matters Most to You

It's time to shine a spotlight on your internal self-Awareness by clarifying where you want to direct your energy.

Fill out the questions and exercises on the following pages to capture what matters most to you. Think of your output as the "sloppy copy." After you finish the Self-Awareness chapter, **I urge you to complete the What Matters Most document using the QR code**. This will serve as your living document that captures what really matters to you. I encourage you to annually review and update it as you make progress and evolve as a leader.

Roles

Identifying your most essential roles helps clarify and focus your attention and time. Consider the roles you currently serve across the various dimensions of your life, both professionally and personally. Parent? Leader? Spouse? Caregiver? Expert in your field? Which roles are the most important to you now? How are they likely to shift over time?

Within our work life, most of us inhabit multiple roles. For example, you might serve as a sales director or financial analyst–your job title. If you are in a leadership role, you might also consider yourself a mentor, a change agent, or a people developer. Perhaps you take your role as a colleague very seriously, wanting to show up as a fantastic team member. Maybe you are committed to allyship for anyone who may feel disenfranchised.

Being a parent, a caregiver, a spouse, or a partner may be a critical role you play in your personal life. You may also serve on a board or be active in your neighborhood association, spiritual community, or sporting team in the community at large.

Your Top Three Roles

List the three most important roles you serve now in order of importance. Examples might include leader, parent,spouse, mentor, student, professional, etc.

1.

2.

3.

Example:

1. Parent to my three children
2. Leader of my organization
3. People developer

ANY THOUGHTS OR OBSERVATIONS? ARE THERE ANY ROLES YOU'RE NOT CURRENTLY SERVING BUT WANT TO IN THE FUTURE? IF SO, HOW WILL YOU MAKE ROOM FOR IT/THEM?

I was a card-carrying workaholic early in my career. Work was my identity and sole focus. While I wanted a family, there was no time to focus on making it happen. Only after my grandmother Mable died did I take a hard look at my life. I remember sitting at her funeral, looking at everyone who filled the pews. So many who had loved and cared about her were her children and their families. My friend's words from earlier that year struck me in a fresh new light. "Your job will never love you back." Her passing was my wake-up call to question how I lived my life. I needed to make room for my future role as a partner and a parent.

-Angie

Once you name your key roles, examine the amount of energy you give each role. For example, if being a mentor to others is vital for you, what are the goals and activities that direct your energy as you fully embrace this part of your life? Does your calendar reflect the importance of the role? Many allow their primary work role to dominate their focus. While this is appropriate during phases of your career, if you only focus on your work role, you may limit your ability to advance essential goals in the rest of your life.

THOUGHTS?

Values

Values serve as our North Stars, guiding our behavior across all the roles we fill. When our values and daily life are congruent, life feels "in the flow." When they're not, life can feel overwhelming as your internal struggle for your sense of self rages on. Keeping our values in plain sight and consciously living into them helps us align with our beliefs and goals.

Consider the values that really influence your decisions and guide your behaviors. Can you rank order your top three values?*

1.

2.

3.

Example:

1. Lifelong learning
2. Being financially secure
3. Integrity

* Of course you'll have more than three values–go ahead and circle or list them on the next page. We are ranking the top three values to help you focus.

The following list may help you get started. Values are deeply personal, so change the words to better capture your essence or write your own.

Honesty and truth

To be part of a meaningful community–belonging

Feeling connected to others

The respect of others

A happy, healthy family

A long life free of illness

Well-being–being emotionally, physically, and spiritually healthy

The courage to act and live by my convictions

Recognition for competence and accomplishments

Respect and dignity

Integrity

Self-development

Lifelong learning

Being open to learning about others

A life of leisure–freedom from work or duties

Being a leader–the ability to guide or direct others

Privacy–being content when alone

A deep and satisfying love with someone

Service to others

Making a difference/creating a legacy

Freedom to be and do what you want in life

Love and admiration of good friends

Adventure

Complete self-confidence

Appreciation of beauty and the beautiful

Possessing a deep and satisfying religious faith

A lifetime of financial security and or/wealth

A beautiful home

Helping to achieve a world without prejudice and cruelty

Being famous or renowned for your achievements

Understanding the meaning of life

Success in your chosen profession

Helping to gain greater knowledge

Being creative and creating things

Security–feeling safe

Have you ever been stuck in a job or company that clashed with your values? It can be exhausting and soul sucking. If you find yourself in this situation, make sure you are clear about what you value before you jump ship so that you don't repeat the pattern.

How roles and values intersect

Now, consider your top roles and your most essential values together. For each role, consider the ways your values play out.

Values by Role

1. Write your roles in the first column and your top three values across the first row.
2. In the blank boxes, describe how your values manifest within each role. That is, how do you see your values show up within each role? So, for example, let's say one of your key roles is "parent," and one of your values is "adventure." In the box intersecting parent and adventure, you might fill in "annual family vacations to new places." See the example below for ideas.

EXERCISE 3 EXAMPLE: VALUES BY ROLE

KEY ROLES	VALUE 1 *Lifelong Learning*	VALUE 2 *Being Financially Secure*	VALUE 3 *Integrity*
1. Parent	*Making sure I bring in new experiences and take family vacations that expose my children to other ways of living.* *I read to my children and talk about the books we are all reading.*	*Teaching my children about money.* *Keep managing the family budget and investing in our future.*	*Being a good role model and talking openly about difficult choices.*
2. Leader	*Challenging my team and organization to learn from our mistakes and keep scanning for more effective ways of doing things.* *I host weekly lunch-and-learn sessions to encourage learning from one another.*	*Managing our department budget effectively. I treat the company's resources as if they were my own.*	*Being impeccable with my words and actions. I want to be known for being transparent and honest with everyone.* *I strive to speak truth to power.*
3. People Developer	*I keep up to date on everyone's career goals.* *Everyone in my organization has an active development plan to help them achieve their goals.*	*I make sure people understand all the financial benefits the company provides.* *My team understands the business and key financial indicators.* *As a team we review and discuss the monthly and quarterly financial results.*	*I try not to shy away from having crucial feedback conversations that will help the people in my organization achieve their individual and our team's goals.*

EXERCISE 3: VALUES BY ROLE

KEY ROLES	VALUE 1	VALUE 2	VALUE 3

DO YOUR MOST IMPORTANT ROLES AND KEY VALUES ALIGN WITH HOW YOU LIVE YOUR DAILY LIFE? ARE YOU LIVING YOUR TOP VALUES AS YOU GO ABOUT LIVING EACH ROLE? IF NOT, WHAT ADJUSTMENTS ARE NEEDED?

This exercise highlights where your values may or may not be showing up in the most critical roles you serve. Why? Because living out each of your critical roles while living harmoniously with your values makes life feel more in sync, especially when life gets hectic and overwhelming.

DID YOU HAVE ANY EMPTY BOXES? IF SO, WHAT ACTIONS COULD YOU TAKE TO BRING THIS VALUE TO LIFE ACROSS ALL YOUR LIFE AND WORK ROLES?

Purpose Statement and Leadership Narrative

If values are the "how," purpose is the "what." Can you articulate a purpose statement that helps define who you are and what you plan to do with your one, juicy life? Having a clear purpose provides inspiration, direction, and clarity. It serves as your filter as opportunities present themselves, steering you away from positions that will force you to compromise your core beliefs or spend time on matters that aren't important to you. It's the red thread that weaves the roles you choose into a congruent, well-lived life.[15]

Before launching into your purpose statement, let's do a quick warm-up exercise. Don't worry about whether it's perfect and all-inclusive.

Taking all the above into consideration, what are the most important goals you hope to achieve over your lifetime? To make it easier, consider breaking your goals into categories such as personal, family/friends, work/school, and community.

EXERCISE 4 EXAMPLE: MOST IMPORTANT GOALS

	BIG LIFE GOALS
PERSONAL	*Run the NYC marathon by the time I'm forty. Travel to all seven continents.*
FRIENDS/FAMILY	*Get married and have children. Be a great role model. Be there for my parents as they get older.*
PROFESSIONAL	*Reach the highest level I can. I want to be in charge of a great organization.*
COMMUNITY	*Get involved and be a leader in my community by volunteering and serving on boards. Get involved in solving homelessness in my community.*

EXERCISE 4 : MOST IMPORTANT GOALS

	BIG LIFE GOALS
PERSONAL	
FRIENDS/FAMILY	
PROFESSIONAL	
COMMUNITY	
OTHER AREAS OF YOUR LIFE THAT ARE ESSENTIAL	

Is there a theme that runs through your high-level goals? In the example above, you might see threads of living into their potential, being open to new experiences, and serving others.

WHAT ARE THE PRIMARY THEMES FOR YOUR HIGH-LEVEL GOALS YOU'LL WANT REFLECTED IN YOUR PURPOSE STATEMENT?

Purpose statement

Your purpose statement is uniquely yours. It should define who you are and motivate you most every day.

Here are some examples:

"My purpose is to leave the world a better place than I found it, through leadership that is both performance-driven and principled." **Indra Nooyi** (former CEO, PepsiCo)

"I strive to serve my country and the global community with pragmatic, principled, and resilient leadership." **Angela Merkel** (former chancellor of Germany)

"To put a ding in the universe." **Steve Jobs** (cofounder of Apple)

"To relieve suffering and to exercise compassion. We are all in this together, for life is a common, not individual, endeavor." **Harry Blackman** (US Supreme Court justice)

MY PURPOSE IS TO . . .

As you draft your statement, consider the following questions:

- Is it bigger than you?
- Does it feel right?
- Will this statement help you focus on what matters most?

It may take a few iterations to land on a purpose statement that truly captures your life's work. Be patient with yourself if it's not evident to you.

Write your draft purpose statement on an index card or on your phone. Carry it around with you and make it visible during your day. Keep editing it until you feel it truly resonates with you.

My leadership narrative

As you think about your purpose statement, also consider the kind of leader you hope to be. Developing your leadership narrative helps establish the impact you want to have on others and the legacy you wish to leave for yourself and those you care about. You can also use this narrative as you transition to new teams or as the backdrop to asking for feedback.

WHAT KIND OF LEADER DO YOU HOPE TO BE?

HOW DO YOU HOPE OTHERS DESCRIBE YOUR LEADERSHIP?

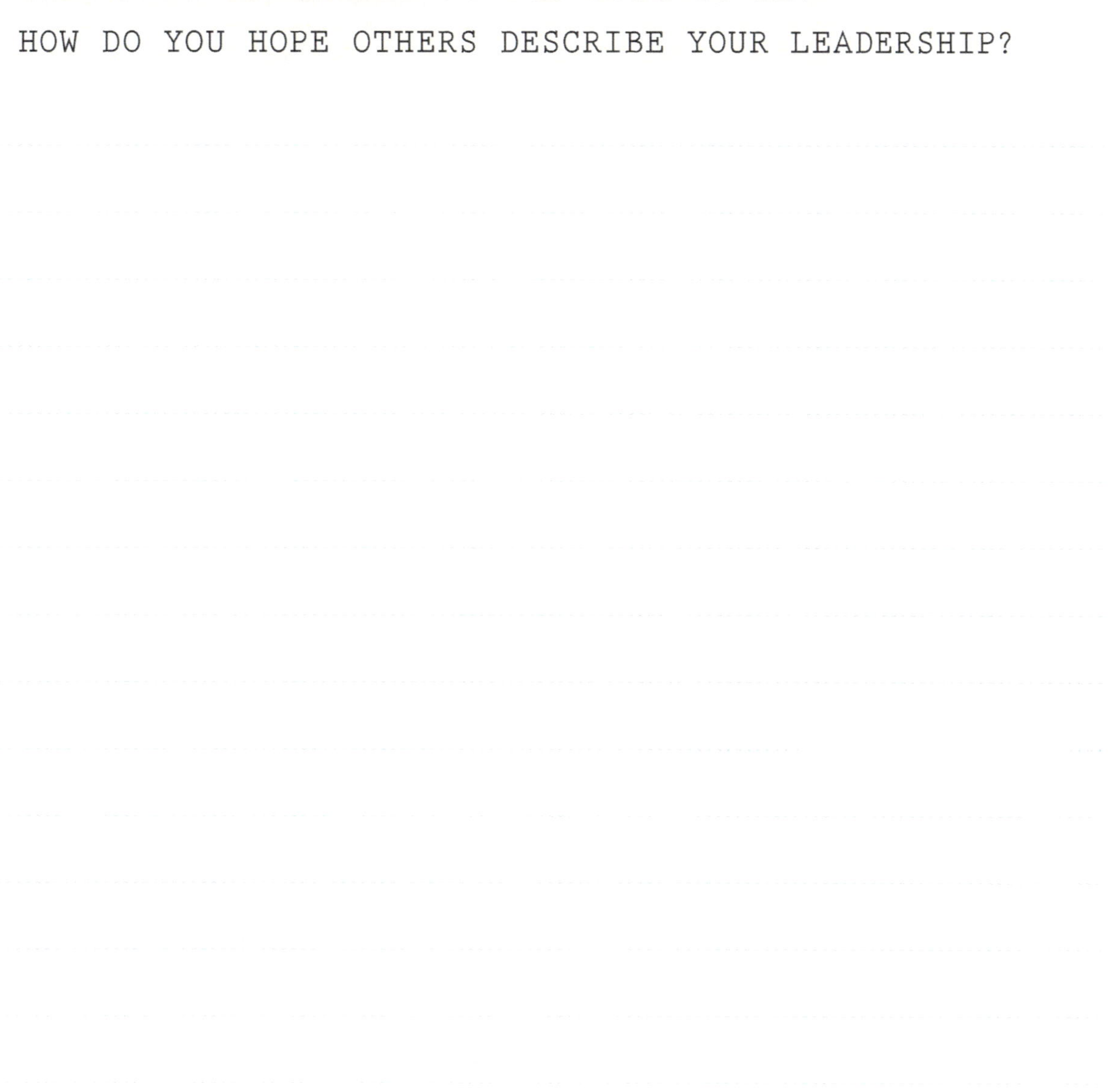

Revisit this statement at the end of the week. Edit your statement to match your aspirations. (Remember it's aspirational and may not reflect how you currently show up as a leader. That's where feedback will help.)

Spotting strengths

Now that you've clarified your roles, values, and purpose, let's move on to the gifts you bring with you on this journey. We all have talents or strengths. Think of these as our superpowers.

The tricky part about strengths is that they come easily to us, so we often take them for granted or assume everyone has similar superpowers.

My mother's family was thick with artists. My grandmother was a talented craftswoman. One son was an architect, the other an artist. Like her mother, my mother could sew, crochet, and pick up any new craft fad that came her way. My siblings had similar wiring. I convinced myself the creative gene had skipped me altogether. It was after I started working professionally that people frequently mentioned my creativity. I love to brainstorm and can't seem to cut off new ideas, connections between two unlike things, and see possibilities in almost everything. It took a few years for me to claim creativity as a strength. My artistry or creativity may not flow on the canvas, drafting table, or crochet needle, but it flows in the world of ideas and possibilities.

> *"You owe it to all of us to get on with what you are good at."*
>
> –**W.H. Auden** (influential poet, writer, Nobel Prize in Literature)

You might have uncovered a strength if...

- You get feedback from others about it. It might come in the form of "Wow, you're really good at [fill in the blank]," or it can show up in the various awards and shout-outs you've received.
- It feels effortless. You don't have to put a lot of thought or work into using it. You find yourself volunteering to use this strength on teams. It helps you accomplish goals you care about. In school, you might have received good grades in the subject.
- It feels fun and rewarding. You feel "in the flow" when you're in the process of using it.

Your standout strengths

Identify your top three strengths based on your self-assessment and any feedback you have received.

Use the list of strengths below to prompt your thinking. Don't worry if your strengths don't show up on this list. Use language and descriptions that ring true for you.

STRENGTHS

STRATEGIC AGILITY: Ability to see the big picture and navigate complex environments

EMOTIONAL INTELLIGENCE: Understanding and managing one's emotions and those of others

DECISION-MAKING ABILITY: Making timely and well-informed decisions

VISIONARY THINKING: Inspiring others with a clear, compelling vision for the future

RESILIENCE: Ability to recover from setbacks and maintain focus

EMPATHY: Understanding and sharing the feelings of others

COMMUNICATION SKILLS: Effectively conveying ideas and information

PROBLEM-SOLVING: Creative and effective solutions to complex challenges

TEAM BUILDING: Creating and nurturing strong, collaborative teams

ADAPTABILITY: Thriving in changing environments and uncertain situations

CONFLICT RESOLUTION: Skill in resolving disagreements and fostering cooperation

DELEGATION: Knowing how and when to assign tasks to others effectively

FINANCIAL ACUMEN: Understanding financial information and using it to make decisions

NETWORKING: Building relationships that advance personal and organizational goals

TIME MANAGEMENT: Efficiently managing time and priorities

MENTORING AND COACHING: Helping others develop and grow professionally

CREATIVE THINKING: Generating new ideas and innovative approaches

RISK MANAGEMENT: Anticipating and mitigating potential risks

INFLUENCE: Persuading and motivating others to align with your vision

NEGOTIATION SKILLS: Reaching mutually beneficial agreements with others

PUBLIC SPEAKING: Effectively delivering presentations to large groups

CONFLICT MANAGEMENT: Navigating difficult conversations and ensuring productive outcomes

ETHICAL DECISION-MAKING: Adhering to high standards of integrity and fairness

CUSTOMER FOCUS: Understanding customer needs and prioritizing their satisfaction

CHANGE MANAGEMENT: Leading and guiding others through organizational change

EXERCISE 5 EXAMPLE: IDENTIFYING STRENGTHS

STRENGTHS	DESCRIPTION
1. STRATEGIC AGILITY	*I'm good at seeing patterns and the big picture. I can easily map tactical steps to strategic initiatives.*
2. FINANCIAL ACUMEN	*I'm well versed in interpreting financial reports. This helps me make better business decisions.*
3. TALENT ASSESSMENT AND DEVELOPMENT	*I have an excellent track record of spotting and developing talent. The hires I've made are typically sought after in the company. My direct reports typically shine relative to their peers.*

EXERCISE 5: IDENTIFYING STRENGTHS

STRENGTHS	DESCRIPTION
1.	
2.	
3.	

HOW CAN YOU BETTER LEVERAGE EACH STRENGTH?

A CAUTIONARY NOTE: Sometimes, we can overuse our strengths to the point of being a vulnerability.[16] For instance, I sometimes find myself overwhelming others with new ideas. I continue to work on honing the timing of when I use this superpower. It's usually helpful at the start of new projects or when solving a novel problem. Creativity can turn into dysfunction when a plan is in execution mode or when too many ideas are attempted without narrowing the focus.

CONSIDER THE DARK SIDE OF YOUR STRENGTHS. HOW MIGHT OVERUSING ONE OR TWO OF YOUR STRENGTHS WORK AGAINST YOU?

Vulnerabilities

On the flip side of strengths, we all have our limitations or vulnerabilities. Vulnerabilities are traits or aptitudes that feel difficult and may often frustrate you. These pesky weaknesses show up in misguided development or improvement plans. Unfortunately, we usually know a great deal more about our flat spots than our strengths. Most feedback systems (performance reviews, grading systems, etc.) emphasize where you might fall short. While it's critical to know our vulnerabilities and where we can improve, it's also essential to understand how working on any vulnerability will impact our goals. Yes, you may be able to bring your weakness to be average or even above average, but will this effort help you move closer to your goals?

Essentially, we need to consciously and carefully choose where we focus our developmental efforts. Spending a great deal of energy to "fix" a weakness may not be the best use of our time. What if we figured out how to minimize our limitations by building compensating systems around us, creating routines or strategies, or using our strengths more powerfully?

What are some vulnerabilities you need to compensate for? Vulnerabilities are traits or skills that feel difficult and may often frustrate you. They may be mentioned in your performance review as areas for development.

Here is a list of vulnerabilities to prompt your thinking. Don't worry if your vulnerabilities don't show up on this list. Use language and descriptions that ring true for you.

VULNERABILITIES

OVERCONFIDENCE: Becoming too certain of one's abilities, leading to risky decisions

LACK OF DELEGATION: Taking on too much responsibility, leading to burnout

INFLEXIBILITY: Being resistant to change and new ideas

AVOIDING DIFFICULT CONVERSATIONS: Hesitant to provide constructive feedback or address conflict. Being conflict adverse.

MICROMANAGING: Struggling to let go of control, undermining trust and team ownership.

OVERCOMMITTING: Taking on too much and struggling to prioritize.

INCONSISTENT COMMUNICATION: Leaving teams confused or uncertain by not communicating clearly or often enough.

ANALYSIS PARALYSIS: Overanalyzing or waiting for perfect information, which slows down decision-making.

PEOPLE-PLEASING: Trying to keep everyone happy, leading to unclear priorities or loss of credibility.

RESISTANCE TO FEEDBACK: Taking feedback personally or ignoring input that could fuel growth.

LACK OF EMPATHY: Failing to tune into others' emotions or perspectives, which damages trust and morale.

FAILURE TO DEVELOP OTHERS: Focusing only on personal performance instead of helping others grow.

EXERCISE 6 EXAMPLE: IDENTIFYING VULNERABILITIES

VULNERABILITIES OR WEAKNESSES	HOW MIGHT YOU COMPENSATE FOR THIS VULNERABILITY? IS THERE A ROUTINE OR STRATEGY YOU CAN PUT IN PLACE TO HELP?
1. DISORGANIZED *I can be disorganized when I'm overly stressed.*	*Stick with my weekly and daily planning routine during stressful times. At the end of the workday, try to keep my desk clear and close tabs and files to keep my digital world organized.*
2. CONFLICT ADVERSE *It's difficult for me to engage in conflict with my peers.*	*Reframe conflict as collaboration. Speak up without getting defensive. Keep reflecting on "Where did I avoid a hard conversation this week? What's one small issue I can address early next week before it grows?"*
3. LOWERED ENDURANCE DURING INTENSE WORK CYCLES *Working late into the night works against me. When I don't get enough sleep, it's difficult for me to function well the next day.*	*Prioritize sleep during the weeknights. Bow out of optional late night work events. Keep to my routine.*

EXERCISE 6: IDENTIFYING VULNERABILITIES

VULNERABILITIES OR WEAKNESSES	HOW MIGHT YOU COMPENSATE FOR THIS VULNERABILITY? IS THERE A ROUTINE OR STRATEGY YOU CAN PUT IN PLACE TO HELP?
1.	
2.	
3.	

Your ideal working environment

There is one last piece of internal self-awareness I'd like you to need to consider. What is your ideal working environment?

Workplace cultures vary widely. Not every work environment will be a good fit for you. That is, culture can impact our ability to thrive as leaders. So, taking the time to articulate your ideal situation can save you time and emotional pain. As you reflect upon your current and past experiences, what conclusions can you draw regarding your ideal working environment? Under what conditions do you feel you can show up authentically and produce your best work? Chances are, it's when you feel supported by your boss and others. What else motivates you?

DESCRIBE YOUR IDEAL WORKING ENVIRONMENT.

ON THE FLIP SIDE, DESCRIBE THE ENVIRONMENTS IN WHICH YOU FEEL THE MOST UNEASY AND UNSURE ABOUT YOUR ABILITIES. IN OTHER WORDS, WHAT'S YOUR KRYPTONITE? WHAT SETTINGS MIGHT BRING OUT THE WORST IN YOU?

REFLECTION

BEFORE MOVING ON TO THE NEXT SECTION, WHAT ARE YOUR BIGGEST AH-HA'S REGARDING YOUR INTERNAL SELF-AWARENESS?

WHAT ARE YOUR NEXT STEPS?

3. Increasing External Self-Awareness: How Others See You

For many, increasing our external self-awareness is often the most painful part of the development journey. Most people struggle with feedback that's less than favorable.

The truth is that feedback is a gift. Without it, we may not know how to get better at what we do, ultimately spending a ton of effort and time that doesn't pay off for us as efficiently or productively as it could be. Become a feedback seeker. Ask for feedback from your manager, peers, or customers. Be specific about the feedback you seek, which helps others help you. Do this often. Rinse and repeat. When someone gives you criticism that could really make a difference in your effectiveness, thank them profusely in the best way you know how. It might have been difficult for them to share it with you, but they cared enough about you to take the risk.

Below are some ways to get high-quality feedback.

- Do a 360 assessment every two years. This assessment gathers feedback from key people you interact with—your boss, direct reports, peers, customers, and other key stakeholders. Responses are kept anonymous, except for your boss. Ask your people/HR team if they provide 360 assessments.
- If you work in a mid to large company, chances are you have access to leadership development programs that include some quality feedback tools. Tap into them.
- If your company doesn't offer any leadership development resources, reach out to an executive coach who can help you gather meaningful feedback.

DIY feedback

If you work for a company that doesn't have a 360-degree process and doesn't have the budget for a coach, here are two quick and easy ways to begin uncovering how others see you.

1. Five-Word Exercise

I picked up this tip from my colleague Greg Clark. Email key people you interact with at work and in your personal life. At a minimum, include your boss, peers, direct reports, and other colleagues who interact with you regularly. The email might go something like this.

> *Subject: Gathering Feedback on My Leadership Style and Effectiveness*
>
> *Hi, team,*
>
> *As part of my commitment to becoming a more effective leader, I'm asking for your honest feedback. Your perspectives are incredibly valuable to me, and I would greatly appreciate your insights.*
>
> *Could you please share the first five words that come to mind when you think about my leadership style and effectiveness? Also, what three strengths stand out to you, and what two areas do you think I could improve or adjust to be more effective?*
>
> *I'd be grateful if you could reply with your thoughts, and I truly appreciate your help as I continue to grow.*
>
> *Thank you in advance for taking the time to provide your input!*
>
> *Best,*
> *[Your name]*

When the email responses come streaming in figure out the common themes. What are the most frequent strengths mentioned? Does this resonate with how you think about yourself? Do any vulnerabilities make it on the list? What adjustments could you make to your leadership approach based on the feedback?

2. Start/Stop/Continue Feedback

The next time you complete a big project or want more feedback from your boss or direct reports, ask the following questions ahead of a face-to-face meeting so that they can give it some thought before you meet.

To [fill in the blank: contribute more, get promoted, take on more responsibility, be more effective, be a more effective leader]:

- What should I *start* doing?
- What should I *stop* doing?
- What should I *continue* doing?

Friends and family

Don't leave out your best supporters—those who love and care about you—as you seek out feedback. Get additional input from those who know you best. They have a front-row seat in your game of life. Pay attention to how their feedback differs from those at work and in other spheres of your life—there may be some subtle overlap worth exploring.

Gaps or blind spots

As you seek feedback, remain aware of potential blind spots—what others notice about us that we may not perceive ourselves. If we're blessed by colleagues and friends who are willing to be honest with us, we can begin to see through and around our blind spots. Research shows that higher-level executives tend to see themselves differently from those around them.[17] Highest ranking leaders often rate themselves more positively than their observers. As they gain power and experience, they may fall prey to inflated views of themselves. This can lead to some pretty spectacular failures.

I once worked with a leader who turned into a raving, egotistical crank when others challenged his ideas. He believed he was always the most brilliant guy in the room. Attempting any healthy debate with this guy was an act of self-flagellation. While he may have been brilliant, the fact that he could not see how his overly argumentative, defensive manner prevented him from working effectively with others. His colleagues started distancing themselves from him, which drove him further into dysfunctional discourse and disruptive behavior. He eventually got fired. Despite multiple attempts by people to show him this glaring blind spot and its impact on others, he could never quite see it. I still wonder what greatness he could have achieved had he only been able to see how he repeatedly got in his own way.

So, the next time someone gives you a piece of feedback you don't think applies to you, slow down and lean in. The harsh light of insight just might be illuminating a blind spot.

Okay, it's time for some fieldwork.

REFLECTION

WHAT APPROACH WILL YOU TAKE TO GETTING FEEDBACK ON HOW OTHERS PERCEIVE YOU? WHAT IS YOUR GAME PLAN? BY WHEN?

WHAT DID YOU LEARN ABOUT YOURSELF BY GETTING FEEDBACK FEEDBACK FROM THOSE YOU RESPECT? REVISIT YOUR STRENGTHS/VULNERABILITY CHART THAT YOU COMPLETED ABOUT YOURSELF. ARE THERE ANY ADJUSTMENTS YOU NEED TO MAKE?

WOW! You've done a ton of work on both internal and external self-awareness. Now complete the following short section on growth mindset to help you thrive through changes.

4. Growth Mindset: Enhancing Your Approach to Change

In the last three sections, we've made the case that increasing your self-awareness is a critical step toward your accelerated development. So, let's take a closer look at one more important piece of the puzzle–your learning/growth mindset.

What was your score on Growth Mindset in the accelerator assessment you took in Chapter 1? Does the score make sense to you?

What is your belief in your ability to learn new skills and evolve as a leader? This belief or mindset is what you actively deploy when facing a change you want or need to make. The key to personal change lies in our willingness to learn about our less-than-perfect selves and be patient enough with ourselves to change.[18] A lack of openness and curiosity can thwart our growth by blaming ourselves, the situation–or worse, other people. It can keep us telling ourselves a reoccurring story about how we're just bad at something and incapable of getting better. This is where having a growth mindset comes magically into play.

Carol Dweck, a Stanford psychologist, uncovered this concept initially in the classroom. She noticed students who believed they could learn something did, while those who believed their abilities were fixed or could not be changed didn't. Students with a growth mindset thought failure was an opportunity to learn, while those with a fixed mindset would rigidly shape their world to prevent mistakes and, God forbid, failure. I encourage you to read Dr. Dweck's book, *Mindset: The New Psychology of Success*. She believes our mindset regarding our ability to change sets people who succeed apart from the rest–not intelligence, talent, or education.

> *"Why waste time proving over and over how great you are, when you could be getting better? Why hide deficiencies instead of overcoming them? Why look for friends or partners who will just shore up your self-esteem instead of ones who will also challenge you to grow? And why seek out the tried and true, instead of experiences that will stretch you? The passion for stretching yourself and sticking to it, even (or especially) when it's not going well, is the hallmark of the growth mindset. This is the mindset that allows people to thrive during some of the most challenging times in their lives."*
>
> **–Carol Dweck**

Check the following statements that may describe you.

EXERCISE 7: GROWTH MINDSET VS FIXED MINDSET

GROWTH MINDSET	FIXED MINDSET
☐ *I believe my essential qualities (talents, IQ, tendencies, etc.) are things I can develop through my efforts, my strategies, and help from others.*	☐ *I believe my qualities (talents, IQ, tendencies, etc.) cannot change.*
☐ *I worry less about looking smart and put more energy into learning.*	☐ *I feel like I'm being evaluated and judged in almost every situation at work. I must keep proving myself, staying ahead of anyone seeing my limited capacity.*
☐ *I believe a person's true potential is unknown, and it's impossible to know what someone can do with years of effort, motivation, and training.*	☐ *I am most concerned with how I'll be judged and don't want to expose any deficiencies.*
☐ *I have a passion for stretching myself, sticking with the effort even when it gets uncertain and uncomfortable.*	☐ *At work, I crave an excessive amount of success and validation.*
☐ *I thrive on getting better at things, often throwing myself into new situations.*	

Neuroscientists are learning that our brains continue to develop throughout our lifetime. We aren't limited to a set number of brain cells we can only lose and never gain. We can regenerate and actively participate in lifelong learning. Whew! Let's take a moment to pause on that concept! (I don't know about you, but this brings me so much hope for myself.) Let's say you've told yourself a story that you are genuinely incapable of speaking confidently in front of large groups. The truth is you can if you are motivated to learn and willing to be uncomfortable as you gain your skills.

WHAT BELIEFS HELP YOU ATTEMPT NEW THINGS? WHAT BELIEFS MIGHT BE HOLDING YOU BACK?

As humans, we experience both growth and fixed mindsets. It's not an either/or concept but on a spectrum. We all move back and forth on the spectrum depending on the challenge, the support around us, and the story we tell ourselves about what's possible. Understanding what triggers your fixed mindset and countering it as soon as you notice it helps get you back to a growth mindset.[19]

WHAT TRIGGERS YOUR FIXED MINDSET?

WHAT DO YOU SAY TO YOURSELF WHEN YOU ARE FACING A NOVEL CHALLENGE?

If your self-talk indicates a fixed mindset, try replacing thoughts of frustration with words like:

- "I can do this. I'm improving with each attempt."
- "Who do I know that's really good at this? I wonder how they learned to do it."
- "What a great opportunity to learn something new."
- "Stop doubting yourself and start doing."
- "Okay, internal critics, time to move on."

A word about fixed mindset environments

Many corporate environments I've experienced feed on people with a fixed mindset. While more progressive companies adopt a growth mindset, many still judge harshly, expecting perfection even when the challenges are novel and ambiguous. If you've ever experienced a performance review process where only a few people could achieve the highest rating, a fixed mindset may be a play. So, you'll want to pay attention to the culture of any potential employer. Ask how they handle performance reviews and leadership development. Look for organizations that support learning vs. perfection.

ON A SCALE OF 1-10, HOW WOULD YOU RATE YOUR CURRENT ORGANIZATION ON THE LEVEL OF GROWTH MINDSET AMONG TOP LEADERS? WHAT EVIDENCE CAN YOU POINT TO?

Another element of maintaining a learning mindset is staying open to new approaches to doing work. Stay curious! Delight in learning what's working for other people in other teams, departments, and companies. Resist the urge to judge new ideas too quickly. When you find yourself jealous of someone, stop and learn from them.

ARE THERE PEOPLE YOU ENVY? WHY? WHAT CAN YOU LEARN FROM THEM?

REFLECTION

BEFORE WE MOVE ON TO CLARIFYING YOUR FOCUS, WHAT ARE YOUR BIGGEST AH-HA'S OR KEY LEARNINGS FROM THIS CHAPTER YOU WANT TO REMEMBER?

Wrap-Up and Next Steps

Congratulations, you have done a ton of work. Hopefully, by completing this chapter, you have clarified what matters to you (roles, values, purpose statement, leadership narrative, strengths, vulnerabilities, ideal working environment) and better understand how people perceive your actions/leadership in the workplace. Hopefully, you are bolstered by the fact that you can learn and change by cultivating a growth mindset. Complete the **What Matters Most worksheet** and keep it as a living document.

In the next chapter, we'll build on your hard work in this chapter and articulate your work and life goals.

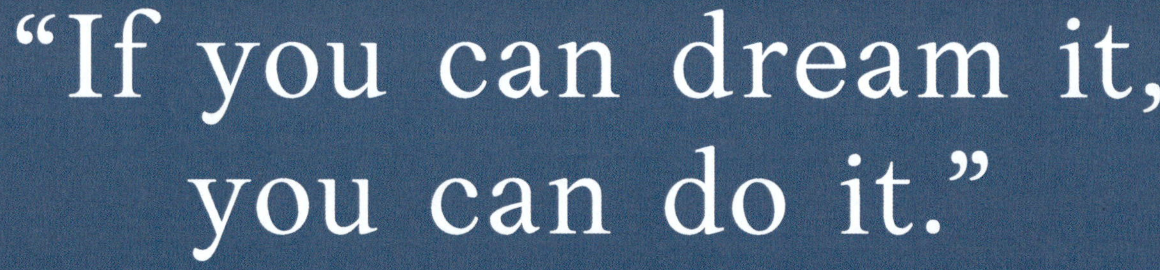

"If you can dream it, you can do it."

–WALT DISNEY (innovator, entertainment pioneer, founder of Disney)

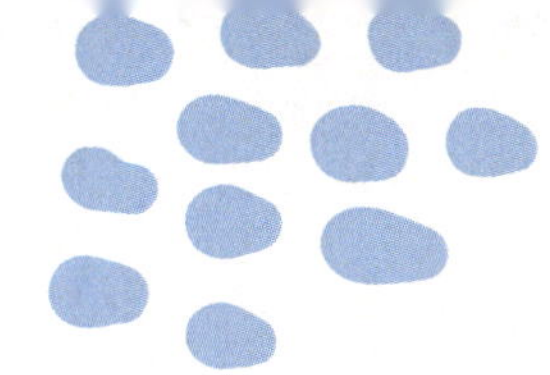

3

HARNESSING THE POWER OF FOCUS

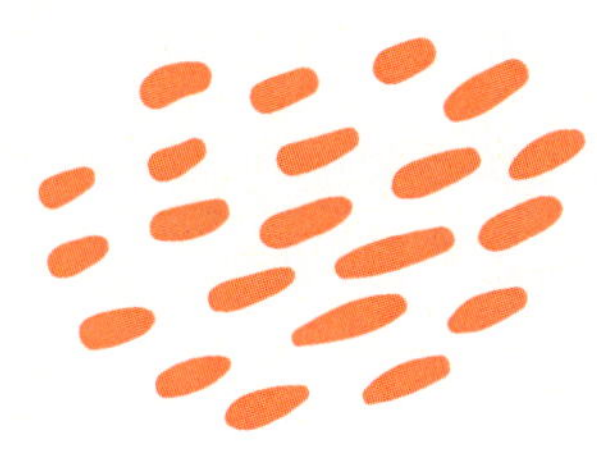

Harnessing the Power of Focus

"You are never given a wish without also being given the power to make it come true."

–**Richard Bach** (author)

In this chapter, we'll dive into the transformative power of focus and how it can elevate your leadership and personal growth. Here's what you'll discover:

1. The Power of Clarity
Learn why setting clear goals not only provides direction but also inspires others to rally behind and support your vision.

2. Intrinsic (and Extrinsic) Motivation
Explore how aligning your goals with your inner drive–competency, autonomy, and connection–keeps you motivated, engaged, and persistent on the path to success.

3. Share Your Goals
Find out how sharing your goals with others boosts accountability, creates opportunities for collaboration, and significantly amplifies your chances of success.

By the end of this chapter, you'll have the tools and insights to sharpen your focus and energize your efforts.

The Power of Clarity

Creating the life you desire requires clarity—a clear direction and purposeful steps forward. For mid-career stallers like Vanessa in our client story on page 64, breaking free from stagnation isn't about working harder; it's about uncovering and validating your dreams and goals, both big and small, personal and professional.

Without clarity, your potential supporters and champions won't know how to help you. They can't advocate for you, nominate you for opportunities, or guide you toward the roles and experiences that align with your vision. Worse, they don't know what feedback to give you to fuel your growth. But when you have a clear direction, everything begins to align. Your goals become the compass that helps you prioritize projects, evaluate opportunities, and decide where to focus your time and energy. It's not just about moving forward—it's about moving forward with purpose.

The big why for having a big why: Goals matter

Setting goals motivates us to move toward our highest hopes and dreams. In a world where anything is possible, it's easy to get overwhelmed by choice. If your palms are getting sweaty at the thought of committing to a direction, know you are not alone.

Overcoming the 'what-if' doubts

Saying "yes" to one path often means saying "no" to many others—and that can feel overwhelming. With so many possibilities, making a choice can feel like closing doors rather than opening them. The "What if you went this way?" voice might whisper in your mind, only to be drowned out by anxiety and second-guessing.

But what if we reframed that voice? Instead of feeling paralyzed, try saying, "Let's go this way for now." Choosing a direction doesn't mean locking yourself into it forever. You can always pivot, adjust, or explore new paths later. Sometimes, progress comes from moving forward—not from agonizing over every potential option.

> *"The best way to predict the future is to create it."*
>
> **—Abraham Lincoln**

A MID-CAREER STALLER

Vanessa was one of those rare individuals who could light up a room with her sharp wit, exceptional charisma, and a great laugh. She was masterful at learning from her experiences and was deeply self-aware. But when she came to me, she was stuck.

"I just don't know what I want," she admitted during one of our early sessions. Her voice carried a mix of frustration and vulnerability. Despite her remarkable ability to solve everyone else's problems, her own path forward felt murky. Vanessa's inner critics were loud, whispering doubts that undermined her confidence. "Who do you think you are?" that inner voice of hers would say. "You're not executive material."

So, I asked Vanessa a direct question: "What do you really want?" She hesitated, offering the kind of vague, safe responses I'd heard before: "I want to contribute" or "to grow." But I wasn't going to let her off the hook.

"Vanessa," I said gently but firmly, "you're not stuck. I wonder if you are just afraid to say what you really want out loud."

She looked at me, startled. For a moment, the room was silent. Then, with a deep breath, she said the words that changed everything: "I want to become a senior leader in this organization." As soon as she spoke those words, something shifted. It was as if a weight had been lifted.

What surprised her most was the reaction from her peers and colleagues later that week. When she shared her aspirations, they didn't question her readiness or capability. Instead, they rallied around her. "You'd be fantastic," one colleague said. Another chimed in, "We've been waiting for you to step into this role." Her boss, one of her biggest fans, broke into a smile. "Finally," he said, "we know how to help you progress."

From that moment forward, Vanessa's trajectory changed. With a newfound clarity of purpose, she began taking deliberate steps toward her goal. She sought out mentorship, embraced challenging assignments, and leaned into visible leadership opportunities. Her inner critic didn't disappear overnight, but it grew quieter as she started proving to herself that she was indeed very capable.

As her coach, I had the privilege of witnessing her transformation firsthand. Vanessa's story is a testament to the power of clarity and courage. When we dare to name our aspirations and invite others to support us, we open doors not only for ourselves but also for those who believe in us.

Define Your Short-Term and Long-Term Goals

Look back at the purpose statement you created in the last chapter. Take a moment to map out your goals for the near future (one to two years) and the longer term (three to five years). Use the matrix below to help clarify your thinking. Go ahead and establish a direction, even if you are a bit unclear about how you'll achieve your goals—clarity on the how will come later.

Below are some examples, and then you'll fill in your goals.

EXERCISE 8 EXAMPLE: EARLY-STAGE CAREER

OVERVIEW OF YOUR BIG GOALS	SHORT-TERM GOALS (one to two years)	LONG-TERM GOALS (three to five years)
Personal	*Better manage my stress. Meditate in the early morning. Run three times a week.*	*Start our family.*
Professional	*Establish myself as an insightful analyst with high potential by overachieving my quarterly goals and taking on more responsibility by the end of the fiscal year.*	*Get promoted to a leadership position within three years and evidentially get selected to be the VP of my division (within the next 10 to 15 years).*

EXERCISE 8 EXAMPLE: LATER-STAGE CAREER

OVERVIEW OF YOUR BIG GOALS	SHORT-TERM GOALS (one to two years)	LONG-TERM GOALS (three to five years)
Personal	*Start an exercise routine three times a week to get stronger and have more energy.* *Get involved in my children's school. Explore my options and commit to an activity by the end of September.*	*Help my children thrive in high school and find their path.*
Professional	*Get promoted to VP of my division in the next promotion cycle.*	*Be an executive team member on the C-suite within 5 years.*

EXERCISE 8: DEFINE YOUR SHORT AND LONG-TERM GOALS

OVERVIEW OF YOUR BIG GOALS	SHORT-TERM GOALS (one to two years)	LONG-TERM GOALS (three to five years)
Personal		
Professional		

TIP: Don't worry about figuring out *how* to achieve your goals just yet. For now, you're simply articulating your goals.

Do your goals genuinely feel like your goals rather than what others expect and want from you?

Many corporate leadership programs assume participants are motivated to get to the next level and never really pause to confirm their assumptions or ask what each participant wants. Don't get caught up in the well-worn path they have created (unless that's what you want). On the flip side, if you don't have clarity on your long-term goals, why not go down the path they have opened for you? It will at least keep you growing and developing until you discover what you want.

Now, get up and take a quick walk before answering the following questions.

As you reflect on the goals you wrote down:

- Do the goals you wrote down feel right? (Are they aligned with your values, purpose, and strengths?)
- Do your goals energize you, or do they make you feel anxious?
- Are your short-term goals slightly out of your reach right now? (We're aiming for challenging but attainable goals.)
- Do your goals genuinely feel like ***your*** goals, rather than what others expect and want from you? (See the sidebar at the bottom of page 66.)

Keep working on your goals until you feel motivated and excited about your short- and long-term intentions.

Intrinsic versus Extrinsic Motivation: Moving Forward from Within

Staying motivated as you work toward your goals often means tapping into your natural, intrinsic motivation. When we're intrinsically motivated, we show up as our most authentic selves—feeling more interested, excited, and confident. This enhances performance, persistence, and creativity, fully engaging our growth mindset.

Intrinsic motivation

Psychologists Richard Ryan and Edward Deci define intrinsic motivation as "the inherent tendency to seek out novelty and challenges, to extend and exercise one's capabilities, to explore, and to learn."[20] We are wired keep developing and expanding our skills and abilities. They identified three core psychological needs that fuel self-motivation. Use this trifecta of motivation to power you forward.

- **Competence or mastery:** The drive to improve in areas we care about—to keep learning and growing. Examples: Becoming an inspirational leader, learning to lead a large organization, or mastering a new language.
- **Autonomy:** The desire to take charge of our own learning journey and choose our path. Many of us need to feel in control of how we work and how we learn. Example: In learning to inspire others, one person might seek out a mentor, another might take a storytelling class, and someone else might embrace challenges that demand inspirational leadership. Some may even do all three.

- **Relatedness or connection:** The need to connect with others and find purpose beyond ourselves. We humans thrive on belonging. Examples include playing a key role in your workplace, knowing your company's product and services improve lives, or coaching your child's soccer team and feeling part of their community.

Extrinsic motivation

Extrinsic rewards (e.g., cash bonuses or promotions) can sometimes undermine natural motivation. For instance, if your boss says, "Get better at storytelling, and I'll give you a bonus," it might shift your focus from the joy of growth to simply earning a reward–it becomes "work."

You might be thinking, "Wait, I really enjoy bonuses and promotions!" And that's valid! Not all extrinsic rewards diminish motivation. In fact, rewards that affirm your competence or align with your values can work hand in hand with intrinsic motivation.

The key is to notice the difference: Think about the last time you learned a skill purely for the joy of it. Now imagine that same skill became a mandatory job requirement–did it feel less exciting? This is why understanding what drives you internally is so important.

EXERCISE 9: EXAMPLES OF INTRINSIC AND EXTRINSIC MOTIVATION

INTRINSIC	EXTRINSIC
Studying for the love of the subject: *You're studying not because you have to, but because you're genuinely curious and passionate about learning more about the subject. The joy of discovering new ideas is your main driver.*	**Studying to get a good grade:** *You're motivated by the external recognition and reward that comes with achieving a high grade. The focus isn't necessarily on learning for its own sake but on the outcome of excelling in a course.*
Working hard on a project because you really enjoy the process: *You thrive on the challenge and satisfaction of creating something meaningful, and the process itself excites you. The sense of accomplishment comes from pushing yourself creatively, not from any external reward.*	**Working hard on a project because you want the bonus once you achieve the results:** *Your primary focus is on earning a financial or professional reward—like a bonus or promotion. The hard work is seen as a means to an end, where the end goal is the tangible reward that follows success.*
Speaking at a conference because you love the topic and are excited to share your knowledge: *You take the stage because you're deeply passionate about the subject matter and want to inspire others. The thrill of sharing what you know with a curious audience is the ultimate reward.*	**Speaking at a conference to enhance your reputation by posting on social media:** *You take on the speaking engagement to boost your personal brand and social recognition. The outcome of gaining followers, likes, and professional validation is your key motivator, rather than the act of sharing knowledge itself.*

REFLECTION

Self-Assessment—Extrinsic versus Intrinsic Motivation

WHEN WAS THE LAST TIME YOU LOST TRACK OF TIME BECAUSE YOU WERE TOTALLY ABSORBED IN THE WORK YOU WERE DOING? WHAT WERE YOU DOING? WERE YOU INTRINSICALLY MOTIVATED?

As you review your personal and professional goals, reflect on the following questions to ensure they align with intrinsic motivators:

MASTERY: ARE YOUR GOALS FOCUSED ON BUILDING SKILLS OR MASTERING SOMETHING YOU'RE PASSIONATE ABOUT? HOW SO?

REFLECTION

AUTONOMY: DO YOU HAVE CONTROL OVER HOW YOU ACHIEVE THESE GOALS? IDENTIFY SPECIFIC WAYS YOU'RE IN CHARGE OF YOUR LEARNING AND YOUR ABILITY TO ACHIEVE YOUR GOALS.

CONNECTEDNESS: DO YOUR GOALS CONNECT YOU TO SOMETHING GREATER THAN YOURSELF? WILL ACHIEVING THEM HELP YOU BUILD MEANINGFUL RELATIONSHIPS OR CONTRIBUTE TO A LARGER PURPOSE?

What adjustments to your goals will increase your intrinsic motivation, if any?

Sharing Your Goals with Others

Once you've clarified and validated your goals, it's time to invite others into your vision for the future. Sharing your goals isn't just empowering–it also boosts your chances of achieving them.[21] Why? Because the right people can provide support, advocacy, and guidance to help you succeed. We'll dive deeper into the people who support you in Chapter 5.

Think about sharing your aspirations with:

- **Your manager and their boss:** They can align opportunities with your goals and support your development.
- **Family and close friends:** These trusted allies will cheer you on and offer encouragement.
- **Mentors, colleagues, or peers:** They may have insights, connections, or opportunities that can move you forward.

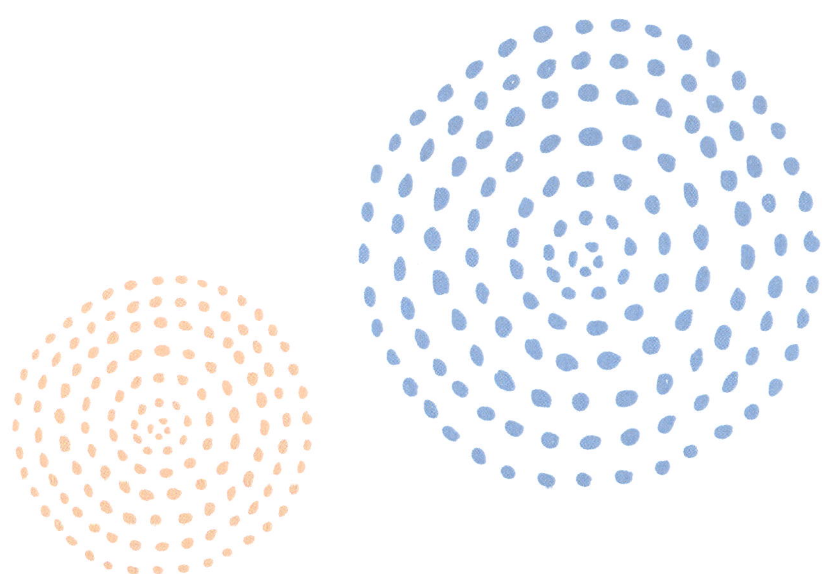

REFLECTION

HOW COMFORTABLE ARE YOU WITH BEING OPEN AND VULNERABLE ABOUT YOUR GOALS?

WHAT'S YOUR STRATEGY FOR SHARING YOUR GOALS WITH KEY PEOPLE LIKE YOUR MANAGER OR THEIR BOSS?

WHO COULD YOU REACH OUT TO FOR GUIDANCE, ADVOCACY, OR INSIGHTS TO HELP YOU SUCCEED?

WHAT NEXT STEP CAN YOU TAKE TO SHARE YOUR GOALS? DO IT NOW.

TAKEAWAY: When you share your goals with others, you create space for unforeseen opportunities to emerge. Your vision begins to take shape in unexpected ways.

Stating your goals out loud to people who can support and guide you can be magical. Once we're clear about our goals, the universe has a funny way of helping us along the way.

Here's an example from my life.
My two trusted business partners and I had been building toward this conversation for months. We had just orchestrated several impactful women's retreats, and now the big question loomed: "What's next?"

As we sat together, reflecting on what we wanted, a sense of both excitement and uncertainty filled the air. We knew we wanted to make a difference—a profound one. Our collective goal was to create a development experience that went deep into self-awareness and offered a long-lasting impact, one that could transform the lives of leaders across the globe. We envisioned something meaningful, something bold. But as we spoke our dreams out loud, we had no idea how or when this vision would take shape.

Two weeks later, the universe answered. My colleague, who worked for a large technology company in Europe, was tasked with developing a unique leadership program—one that would delve into deep self-awareness and spark meaningful, transformational growth. As she described the project, my heart raced. It was exactly what we had envisioned weeks before.

For the next eighteen months, my partners and I worked with her to design and implement the very program we had dreamed of. It became a deeply impactful experience for leaders across Europe. The synchronicity of it all still amazes me.

-Angie

When Others Decide Your Fate

Many leaders set goals that require others to make decisions about their advancement, whether selecting them for a promotion or offering new opportunities. For example, you might aspire to a goal such as "I want to be promoted to vice president within two years" or "I'm aiming for a C-suite position in the next five years." Rest assured, several people will be involved in this decision.

So, once you've defined your goals, it's crucial to understand two things:

- **The requirements** of the role or level you're aiming for
- **How decision-makers view you** and whether you meet or exceed their criteria

This clarity helps you identify gaps, take strategic action, and position yourself for success.

REFLECTION

IF YOUR GOAL REQUIRES OTHERS TO MAKE A CALL ON YOU, HOW WELL DO YOU UNDERSTAND THE REQUIREMENTS OF THE ROLE OR LEVEL YOU'RE TARGETING?

WHAT CRITERIA WILL DECISION-MAKERS USE TO EVALUATE CANDIDATES?

REFLECTION

WHO ARE THE KEY DECISION-MAKERS, AND WHAT STEPS CAN YOU TAKE TO GET ON THEIR RADAR? WHAT'S THE CURRENT PERCEPTION OF YOU AMONG THIS GROUP?

WHAT'S YOUR NEXT STEP IN UNDERSTANDING THE CRITERIA AND PROCESS FOR MAKING YOUR GOAL HAPPEN?

"All that is gold does not glitter,
Not all who wander are lost.
The old that is strong does not wither,
Deep roots are not reached by the frost."

–J. R. R. Tolkien (author of *The Lord of the Rings*)

Finding Your Direction When You Feel Uncertain

If you're unsure about your goals, don't panic. Uncertainty is part of the process. The key is to take action, even if it's small, to discover the path that feels right for you. Here are some steps to guide you.

- **Talk with people doing work that inspires you.**
  Who do you know who is in a role you admire? Search LinkedIn or your personal network to find people doing work you find intriguing. Reach out for a conversation–most people are happy to share their experiences and advice.

- **Reach out to a career counselor or resource expert.**
  Your alma mater's career services office likely has resources available for alumni, even years after graduation. Alternatively, visit your local library. Librarians are experts at helping you uncover tools, information, and connections you might not have considered.

- **Dive into relevant books for inspiration and guidance.**
  Here are a few recommendations to help you find clarity:
  - *Designing Your Life: How to Build a Well-Lived, Joyful Life* by Bill Burnett and Dave Evans–Stanford professors who offer practical tools to design a life you love.
  - *What Color Is Your Parachute?* by Richard N. Bolles–A timeless classic for career exploration and reinvention, continuously updated since 1975.
  - *It's Never Too Late to Begin Again: Discovering Creativity and Meaning at Midlife and Beyond* by Julia Cameron–Ideal for those navigating midlife transitions and searching for their "what's next."

- **Find inspiration in everyday life.**
  Pay attention to moments that ignite your curiosity, interest, or excitement. Record them in a journal or notebook to identify patterns and new ideas over time.

So, if you feel like you're on a "big wander," embrace it with curiosity, intention, and a growth mindset. By taking small, deliberate steps, you'll uncover the direction that's right for you. Remember: the journey itself is part of the discovery process. Keep moving forward and enjoy the adventure.

Wrap-Up and Next Steps

Congratulations on refining your focus. The path ahead may not always feel easy–stepping out of your comfort zone into new territory can be challenging. Keep your goals front and center, and take a few moments each day to visualize the life you're creating. Remember, progress is built one step at a time.

In the next chapter, we'll explore how to turn your on-the-job experiences into powerful opportunities for development. You'll learn how to harness everyday challenges and successes to fuel your growth and bring your goals to life. Let's keep moving forward together!

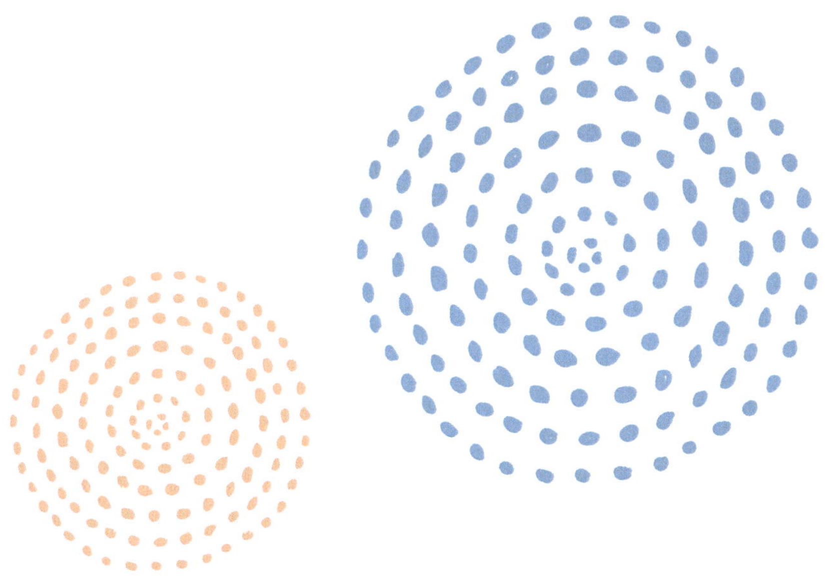

“The only source of knowledge is experience.”

–COMMONLY ATTRIBUTED TO ALBERT EINSTEIN
(genius physicist, innovator, curious, visionary, iconoclastic)

EXPERIENCES THAT CHANGE YOU

Experiences That Change You

"Life is a succession of lessons which must be lived to be understood."

–Commonly attributed to Ralph Waldo Emerson (poet, lecturer, influential essayist)

In this chapter, we'll highlight the importance of experience and share some tools you can use to get the most out of what life and work may bring.

1. **Experience is our best teacher.**
While training events, mentorship, and reading are important, true growth happens when we apply what we've learned in real, high-stakes situations.

2. **Seek out challenging assignments and situations.**
Your most significant growth occurs when the stakes are high, resources are limited, and results are clearly measurable.

3. **Increase your learning agility.**
It's a more significant predictor of leadership success than emotional intelligence or IQ.

4. **Develop a reflection practice.**
Reflecting on your experiences is crucial to distilling the lessons that will help you grow as a leader.

By the end of this chapter, you'll know how to identify high-impact experiences to help you grow, and you'll hopefully be motivated to move on from jobs that no longer challenge you.

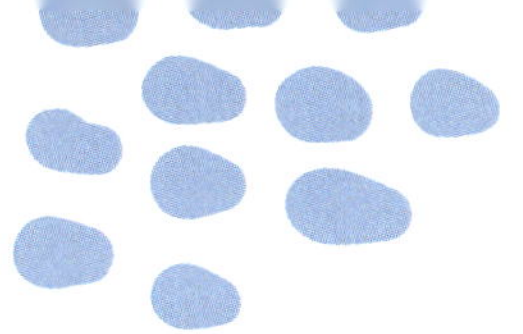

Experience Is Our Best Teacher

Experience is often the toughest–and most rewarding–teacher. Research shows that experience accounts for about seventy percent of your growth as both a professional and a leader. It's the fastest route to mastery, but it doesn't always come easily.[22] Rest assured, it's our most expedient path to growth.

> *"Everything you've ever wanted is sitting on the other side of fear."*
>
> –**George Addair** (20th-century real estate developer, motivational speaker)

LESSONS OF EXPERIENCE

Nancy balanced her two-year-old on her lap, her voice triumphant with excitement as she made the call. "I got the job!" she exclaimed. I could feel the joy radiating through the phone. She had reached a major milestone in her career—a moment that was worth every ounce of celebration.

Nancy's leadership potential had always been undeniable. She possessed a rare combination of intelligence, charm, and a fierce courage that made others gravitate toward her. And she worked with a relentless drive, giving everything she had to her teams. After starting at the company right out of college, she'd worked her way up through the ranks with steady determination. She had successfully led teams before, but this new role was something different. She had just been promoted to vice president at a global technology company, stepping into a leadership position with even more responsibility. It was more than a step forward—it was a leap into a very different world. Now, she was tasked with leading an organization of leaders, each with their own teams, spread across the globe. The expectations were higher, the stakes were greater, and the responsibilities stretched far beyond anything she'd managed before. But Nancy was up for it. It was time to step into a new level of leadership.

But no matter how much she had prepared, no training or structured leadership program could substitute for the lessons that only real-world experience could provide. In this new role, Nancy knew one thing for sure: Growth at this stage wasn't just about learning; it was about leaping—taking bold strides into unfamiliar territory and making the most of every twist and turn.

As Nancy stepped into her new role, she embraced the truth that leadership wasn't about having all the answers. It was about learning. It was about every mistake, every setback, and every success along the way. It was about adapting, reflecting, and growing—sometimes in ways she least expected. The journey ahead would be tough, but with every challenge, she would become the leader she aspired to be, one courageous step at a time.

Make the Most of Your Experiences

Take a moment and think back to a time in your career when you were truly stretched—learning, growing, and navigating something risky. The pressure was on, wasn't it? You likely didn't have all the resources or support you needed. But despite the obstacles, this experience was crucial to your advancement. You and your team may have faced tight budgets, time constraints, or insufficient staff, but you did it. Or perhaps you didn't do it perfectly, but you learned something invaluable along the way, and hopefully you made a significant contribution to the organization.

Now, let's take that reflection further. Research confirms that the most meaningful, impactful growth happens when:

1. **The stakes are high.** Remember the tension when you were working on something that could make or break your team's success? That extra emotional charge—when the outcome mattered not just to you, but to your entire team or organization—had a powerful effect on your ability to push through. These moments are where you become a true leader—navigating both success and failure, driving innovation, and finding solutions when it feels like there's no way forward.
2. **Resources are limited.** This is where innovation happens. When budgets are tight, time is scarce, and the pressure is on, that's when you discover just how creative, resourceful, and resilient you can be. The Plato-inspired proverb "Necessity is the mother of invention" couldn't be more true. These challenging assignments are a goldmine for problem-solving and stretching your skills in new, often uncomfortable, ways.
3. **Results are measurable.** There's nothing quite as rewarding—or as impactful—as seeing clear results from your efforts. Whether it's hitting a revenue target, completing a crucial project, or securing a big win for the company, measurable outcomes provide undeniable proof of your success. And with visible, unambiguous results, your achievements are harder to dispute.

"Smooth seas do not make skillful sailors."

—African proverb

Revisit a period in your career when you were learning and growing the most. You likely felt the pressures and challenges of achieving something risky, yet the experience was crucial to your advancement.

DESCRIBE THE SITUATION. WHAT WAS AT STAKE (FOR YOU AND THE BUSINESS)? WHAT RESOURCES WERE MISSING OR LIMITED? TO WHAT EXTENT WERE THE RESULTS MEASUREABLE? WHAT DID YOU LEARN FROM THIS EXPERIENCE? WHAT WOULD YOU DO DIFFERENTLY NOW, GIVEN WHAT YOU KNOW?

Learning Agility

Most workplaces are ripe with opportunities to learn and grow, which may initially appear as insurmountable roadblocks, exciting possibilities, or fire-breathing crises. The trick is to recognize these moments (or extended periods, in some cases) for what they are and reframe them as extraordinary openings to help transform you and others you care about, such as other team members or your direct reports.

Like Nancy, no amount of preliminary reading or research can prepare you for the first time you attempt a risky or bold move. The gift of experience is in the doing—applying what we think might work, while moving out of our comfort zone. ***Learning only happens when we're uncomfortable.***[23] Growth doesn't come from playing it safe or sticking to the familiar. It happens when we push through the discomfort, embrace trial and error, and keep going until the task is complete. And, just as importantly, growth comes when we reflect on our experiences, taking stock of the lessons we've learned along the way.

Reframe challenging problems and assignments as amazing learning experiences.

"There is no failure. Only feedback."

—Robert Allen (entrepreneur, author, wealth-building expert)

Start with defining what you need to learn at this moment. Being intentional about the skills or mindset you need to rise to the challenge is essential. Whether it's navigating an obstacle or seizing an exciting opportunity, these moments are fertile ground for learning. By reframing challenges—be they roadblocks, setbacks, or high-pressure projects—as opportunities to develop, you open the door to powerful growth. That's where **learning agility** comes into play.

Lombardo and Eichinger originated the phrase, defining it as our ability and willingness to learn from experience and apply those lessons to novel situations. Over the years, psychologists have established that **learning agility is more predictive of leadership potential and performance than emotional intelligence or IQ.**[24] And the good news is that we can improve our Learning Agility over time, meaning that we can learn our way to becoming the leader we hoped to be.

Here's what agile learners do as they gain experience:

- **Embrace discomfort:** They admit they don't know everything and need help from others. Most people will gladly jump in and help if you're open to learning.
- **Observe and reflect:** Reading the room and others, they look for clues on how to proceed. They ask questions like, "What's going on here? What's working and not working? What can I learn here? They make sense of it all. At the same time, they are aware how they are reacting and how they can best meet the moment.
- **Experiment and iterate:** They explore different approaches to solving problems, watching what sticks. They connect the dots to other experiences and situations. They fail fast and learn from it.
- **Adapt:** They are curious and eager to learn new approaches. They love change and seek out new innovations.
- **Open-minded:** They enjoy interacting with and learning from a diversity of people.
- **Driven by getting results:** They are motivated by challenging assignments. They track their efforts, evaluate progress, and adjust strategies accordingly, course correcting as needed.
- **Highly self-aware:** They understand themselves (both internal and external self-awareness) and seek feedback to improve.
- **They think critically and strategically:** They focus on the broader context, bringing multiple perspectives to solve complex problems.

REFLECTION

AS YOU LOOK AT THE LIST OF WHAT AGILE LEARNERS DO, WHAT BEHAVIORS ARE YOU CURRENTLY DOING? WHAT COULD YOU DO MORE OF?

HOW COMFORTABLE ARE YOU WITH BEING "UNCOMFORTABLE" AS YOU ARE LEARNING IN THE WORKPLACE?

HOW WOULD YOU RATE YOUR LEARNING AGILITY? WHAT'S ONE THING YOU COULD START DOING TO HELP BOOST IT?

Seek Out Challenging Experiences That Take You Beyond Your Comfort Zone

As you look back on your career, some experiences will stand out more than others for accelerating your growth. The most impactful experiences aren't the easiest ones–they often involve stepping outside your comfort zone. Below are four high-impact experience types that will stretch your thinking, fuel your learning, and fast-track your development:

1. **The stretch assignment:** Navigating challenging experiences/assignments
2. **Collecting challenging**, varied assignments (cross-functional moves)
3. **Expanding your current role**
4. **Forging your own path and experiences**

The key to wringing out every last drop of learning from an experience is to try to view significant moments in our lives as a series of opportunities, all of which can increase our return on experiences, or ROE.

"Change is not a threat, it's an opportunity. Survival is not a goal, transformative success is."

–**Seth Godin** (author, marketer, entrepreneur)

1. The stretch assignment: Navigating challenging experiences/assignments

"A mind stretched by a new experience can never go back to its old dimensions."

–Inspired by Oliver Wendell Holmes, Sr. (the 19th-century American physician, poet, and polymath and father of Oliver Wendall Jr., a Supreme Court justice)

One of the fastest ways to accelerate your growth is to take on a stretch assignment or dive into a tough, impromptu situation that matters to your team. It's about stepping out of what feels safe and finding challenges that will push you forward and spark new learning. If you keep playing it secure and stick to your comfortable groove, you'll stagnate–and years from now, you might find yourself wondering why you're not further along.

The school of hard knocks is just that–*hard*. But guess what? This is exactly where the magic happens. We all encounter these moments when we push ourselves beyond our limits. Sure, sometimes we face terrifying outcomes: a public failure, an unexpected crisis, or a cringe-worthy mistake. The difference is in how we handle these "opportunities." Do we let them break us, or do we use them to fuel our growth?

Examples of stretch assignments:

- An international assignment
- A turnaround situation
- Starting a new team or department
- Leading a cross-functional team to solve a critical issue for the business

Research shows that the true mark of great leaders isn't the number of mistakes they make; it's the ability to learn from them. Every failure, every misstep, is a lesson in disguise–an opportunity to turn a challenge into a hard-won success. As my colleague Alison Eyring brilliantly puts it in *Pacing for Growth: Why Intelligent Restraint Drives Long-Term Success*, "It's irritating, but the outcome could become a beautiful pearl."[25]

So, the next time you're faced with a gnarly challenge (and we both know it's coming), reframe it as what my husband calls an AFGO–another e'ffing growth opportunity. Embrace the discomfort and get ready for some tuition-free education. Trust me, you'll come out the other side stronger and wiser.

Take a moment to step back and assess your current work situation. Ask yourself these key questions to gauge whether you're truly growing or if you've slipped into your comfort zone:

- **Are you still learning from your manager, colleagues, and clients?** Consider whether you're gaining new insights from those around you or if you've stopped seeking feedback.
- **Are you still gaining necessary experience in your profession or in a new functional area?** Reflect on whether your role still provides opportunities to learn or if it has become repetitive without new challenges.
- **Are you still connecting with people who can help you throughout your career?** Building a network of support is vital. Have you cultivated meaningful connections that will push you forward?

If the answer is "no" to two or more of these questions, it may be time for a change. The red flag of being in your comfort zone is flying high.

Taking Action

If your personal life is not undergoing major transitions (e.g., a newborn, moving to a new home, or heavy caregiving responsibilities), it might be time to consider new opportunities or career challenges. Staying stagnant can hold you back from your full potential–take action before it becomes harder to make the change.

WHAT IS THE MOST IMPORTANT MOVE FOR YOU TO TAKE TO GET OUT OF YOUR COMFORT ZONE?

What to Do When You Find Yourself in an AFGO (Another E'ffing Growth Opportunity)

Take a deep breath. Yes, things are messy, but this is where the most meaningful growth happens. Here's your game plan for navigating this challenge and turning it into an incredible learning experience:

1. **Assess the situation.**
    - What do you know? Start with what's clear. How do you know your information is solid? Verify the facts before making any moves.
    - What don't you know? This is where curiosity is your best friend. What are the gaps? Is there a way to better understand the situation?
    - Who can help fill in the blanks? Identify key players who can provide insight. Seek them out.
    - What documents or records do you need? Are there any files, emails, or notes that will provide clarity?
    - Can you create a timeline? Visualizing the sequence of events might help you see the bigger picture.
2. **Who's in your corner?** Who can support you through this AFGO? Your boss, mentor, and/or your team? Don't try to tackle this alone–gather your allies.
3. **Clarify the goal.** Given what you know now, ask yourself:
    - What must be done immediately? Identify the critical actions that will resolve the situation.
    - What can be put on hold? Recognize what doesn't need your attention right now.
    - How will you know when the situation is under control or resolved? Set clear markers for success.
    - Who are your key stakeholders? Who will judge the outcome(s)? List the people, teams, or groups who are impacted by the situation and will evaluate the resolution. How will you keep them updated?
4. **Stay focused.** Stick to your plan! Don't let distractions or emotional reactions sidetrack you. Continue assessing, revisiting your strategy, and pushing forward.
5. **Communicate.** Keep your key stakeholders informed until the situation is resolved.

Self-Care: The Fuel for High Performance

All this talk of AFGOs, stretch assignments, and getting out of your comfort zone leads me to another important aspect of your development. Let's talk about self-care.

Jim Loehr, a performance psychologist, studied elite athletes. After years of success with athletes, he started applying peak performance athletic principles to corporate leaders, thus coining the phrase "corporate athlete."[26] Elite athletes train hard, pushing their minds and bodies to the limit, but then they rest and restore themselves after high-intensity workouts and competitions. Loehr argues that corporate athletes, just like elite athletes, need downtime to recover and recharge. For example, imagine yourself doing high-intensity work over forty years of your corporate life without ever pausing or taking a vacation. If you fail to recover between "sprints," the probability of you burning out or getting sick increases dramatically. Working on your resilience is key to sustained performance.

In times of high stress, it's easy to forget to take care of ourselves. But here's the truth: You are your primary caretaker–and if you don't take care of yourself, you can't expect to bring your best to work (or life).

After a high-intensity work event or scenario, try to press "pause" so that you may reflect and recover. It will be good for your health, and it will help you come back more mentally prepared to tackle the next big task or slay the next dragon.

So, let's talk specifics. Here are a few things I recommend:

- **Take time off when needed.** High-intensity work cycles are inevitable, but taking a break when it's over isn't just a luxury–it's necessary. When you push hard, you need to pause hard, too. Reflect, recharge, and come back with more energy to tackle the next challenge.
- **Sleep is non-negotiable.** Don't skimp on it. It's not just for recharging–it's for maintaining clarity, focus, and creativity. So, make sure you're getting enough rest, and if you're not, make it a priority.
- **Hydration and nutrition matter.** What you put into your body directly impacts how you show up. Eat well and hydrate consistently, even if it's inconvenient.
- **Disconnect from the digital world.** Set aside time to turn off your devices. Step away from your phone and computer. Trust me, the world won't fall apart in 30 minutes. Disconnecting helps you reconnect to your body and mind.

And don't forget the power of laughter and joy. Life's tough enough without forgetting to enjoy it. So, make space for things that make you smile–whether that's watching a comedy, hanging out with friends, or diving into a hobby you love. Laughter releases endorphins and keeps your spirit light, so why not use it to your advantage?

In short, self-care isn't just a box to check. It's a strategy for keeping yourself mentally sharp, physically energized, and emotionally balanced. The work is hard, but you are the key to staying in the game. Only *you* are the master of your body and mind.

Make ongoing self-care a priority.

2. Collecting challenging, varied assignments (cross-functional moves)

For most of us, not every moment is a high-stakes learning opportunity. So what do you do when you find yourself in a routine job, in the same department, tackling the same tasks with no challenge in sight? Here's a thought: It might be time to shake things up. If you're climbing the ladder or simply hungry for growth, it's worth considering how you can broaden your learning experiences.

Now, let me make a case for expanding your experience horizontally rather than just climbing that vertical corporate ladder. Here's the problem: Many ambitious professionals

A CAUTIONARY TALE OF TAKING THE VERTICAL PATH

Gail, a senior marketing consultant in a growing technology company, had her sights on being promoted to communications director—an executive position. She had started with the company right out of college and had advanced quickly to her current position. She knew everything there was to know about how the team operated. When her boss got tapped to take on another role, Gail was sure she would be asked to lead the team, but she was devastated to learn she had selected someone outside the company to fill the position. The marketing VP (and key decision-maker) had concerns Gail's experience wasn't broad enough to allow her to navigate higher-level issues in the organization and grasp how all the teams worked together to deliver for their customers. The VP also suspected the team's work needed streamlining and worried Gail did not have broad enough experience to navigate those changes. She did not want to set her up for failure, but at the same time, she had not recognized the need for Gail's development sooner—a miss on her part. Gail could have been placed in another assignment outside of marketing to broaden her perspective. Perhaps she would have been better equipped to step into the lead role. Maybe she could have requested the lateral move herself—yet another cautionary tale of why you must take active ownership of your career and development.

get caught in the trap of waiting for that coveted promotion—only to find themselves stuck when a new opportunity doesn't materialize, or someone from another team swoops in as in Gail's case. What's the issue? You may have a wealth of experience in one area, but you must broaden your skills to grow. You might be passed over because you don't have the diverse, cross-functional experience that's needed to navigate leadership at a higher level.

Vertical vs. Horizontal Development

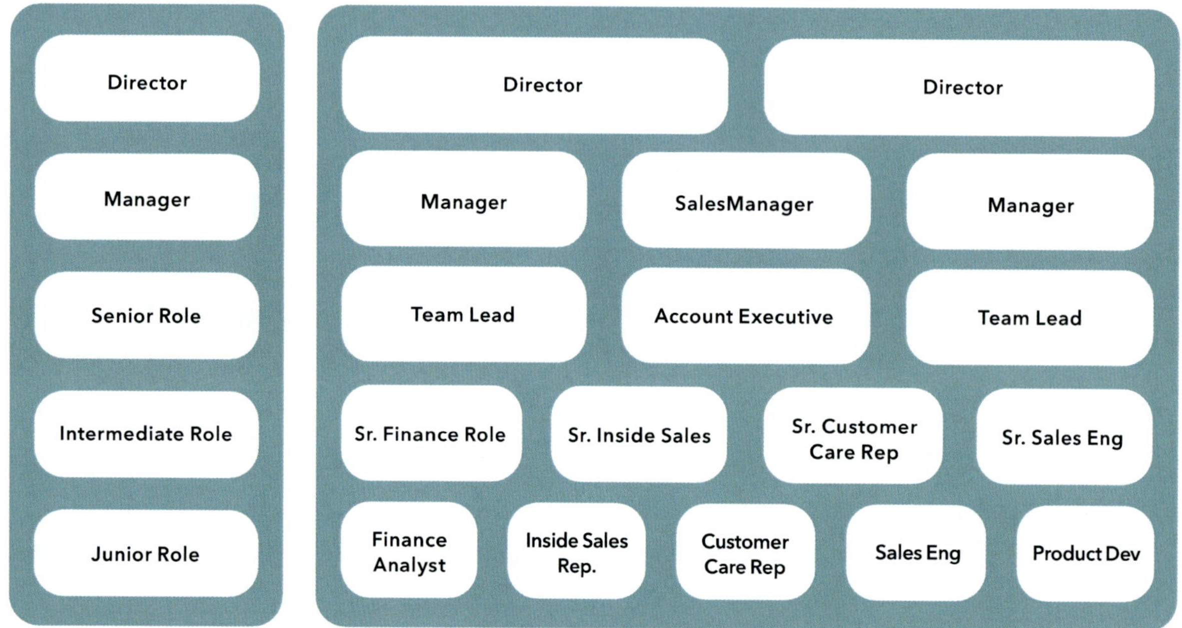

Horizontal movement helps round out your experience.

So, how do you avoid this stagnation? Take a horizontal approach, expanding your view beyond your current role. If you're stuck in a narrow silo, consider what you can do to gain a broader understanding of the business. Talk to your manager about the role you want and make sure they see you as a viable candidate. If that opportunity is still out of reach, consider other ways to broaden your perspective, either by taking on a cross-functional assignment or broadening your scope within your current role. Either path can unlock new opportunities and sharpen your leadership muscles.

If you've been in a role for more than two years and are not growing, it may be time to move on to a different position. If you're happy with your company but feel like your current role isn't offering enough challenges, it's time to explore other departments. Moving laterally can be a powerful way to expand your skill set and broaden your impact. Read Barbara's story on page 94. If your company already offers job rotation programs, make sure you take advantage of those opportunities. If not, why not create your own? Think of it like adding stamps to your "passport" of experience.

REFLECTION

If you're feeling stuck in a job and your comfort zone, consider these questions:

GIVEN YOUR SHORT AND LONG-TERM GOALS, WHAT CROSS-FUNCTIONAL ASSIGNMENT(S) WOULD ENHANCE YOUR LEADERSHIP EXPERIENCE AND DEEPEN YOUR KNOWLEDGE OF THE ORGANIZATION?

- What departments or areas of the business would provide you with a fresh perspective and challenge your current skill set?
- What value would you bring to another team?
- How might stepping into a new area help you grow as a leader?

WHO CAN YOU SPEAK WITH TO GET MORE INFORMATION?

(SOMEONE IN THE ROLE? HR? YOUR MANAGER? YOUR MENTOR?)

- How can you leverage your network to learn more about potential cross-functional opportunities?
- Who in your organization can offer valuable insights or advice on making a lateral move?

THE GOODNESS OF CROSS-FUNCTIONAL MOVES

Barbara was a gifted artist and creative person. Still, when her new family needed a steadier income, she transitioned to a role as a customer service representative at a software company. She became the go-to person when customers were stuck using the product—helping them navigate challenges with a calm and confident demeanor. But Barbara wasn't just quick to learn the ropes; she adapted and excelled, quickly moving into a supervisory role, then to management.

After a few years, though, she felt unfulfilled. She knew she needed something new, something bigger. So, she took the initiative. Reaching out to the HR VP (yours truly), she asked, "What's next for me?" I dug into her long-term career goals, and she responded, "I think I want to be a leader responsible for something big." That was the moment I knew—it was time for her to take on a new challenge, something to broaden her horizons.

Barbara made a bold move to the sales team, conducting product demonstrations—a leap into uncharted waters. She thrived. But what really set her apart wasn't just her performance; she began to play the role of translator and bridge-builder between departments, fostering collaboration across teams. She went from inside sales to becoming an account executive. Now, she's leading a sales team, driving growth and success at a higher level.

Barbara's journey demonstrates that taking on cross-functional roles not only accelerates your personal development, it also allows you to bring immense value to the organization.

A NOTE ON TIMING: Moving cross-functionally is much easier in lower-level roles. As you move up in the organization, it will get harder to find cross-functional experiences without moving backward. So, if it is still early in your career, take advantage of opportunities to change roles across different departments.

3. Expanding your current role

There may be good reasons you cannot move to a new assignment. Perhaps you are covering for a colleague on leave or driving critical projects. It may be time to step up and take on more. Work with your manager to find opportunities to challenge yourself within your current role. Maybe it's streamlining processes, delighting customers in new ways, or solving a pressing company-wide issue.

If you're eyeing a future in leadership, why wait? Ask your manager if you can take the reins as the go-to person when the manager is out, or help recruit fresh talent and mentor the next generation. By expanding your role, you're not just growing—you're preparing for the next big step in your career.

REFLECTION

IF YOU ARE NOT ABLE TO MOVE ON JUST YET, WHAT IDEAS DO YOU HAVE FOR EXPANDING YOUR CURRENT ROLE?

WHAT'S YOUR PLAN TO MEET WITH YOUR MANAGER TO DISCUSS YOUR IDEAS AND GET HIS/HER IDEAS?

4. Forging your own path and experiences

While many people thrive working in the well-worn career paths that often come with more established businesses, this is not for everyone. Many of the entrepreneurs I've worked with over the years are squarely *not* in this camp. They find these paths too restrictive for their passion for creating or trying new ideas. In addition, the pace and management style may not support their unique strengths and often illuminate their non-conformist ways.

Paul was on the brand management track at one of the world's leading consumer products companies. With his innovative ideas and boundless energy, he quickly outgrew the rigid communication protocols that stifled creativity. When his boss delayed Paul's big idea for too long, Paul broke the company's cardinal rule by bypassing his boss and boss' boss–going directly to upper management. The result? The hierarchy came down hard, dismissing the big idea and reinforcing the "we do things this way" mentality. Shortly thereafter, Paul left the company and became a wildly successful serial entrepreneur. By creating companies that embraced innovation and allowed him to amplify his strengths, he found a path that truly matched his passion. Working in a slow-moving company with well-worn career paths, strict top-down communication channels, and loads of bureaucratic rules would never have achieved the goal of tapping into his brilliance and potential.

If this approach resonates with you, it may be time for your entrepreneurial spirit to step out of the corporate world and onto the less-traveled path. As you contemplate this shift, seek out your community of creators and innovators. The great news is that there are plenty of resources–new venture incubators and groups–that are eager to help you on your journey.

Check out valuable resources on my website to help you take the first step.

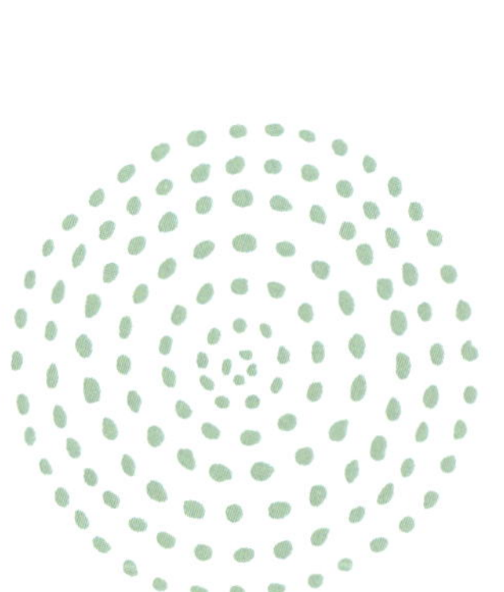

REFLECTION

If you are hearing the entrepreneurial call, consider these questions:

WHO CAN YOU SPEAK WITH WHO HAS TAKEN THIS PATH?

- What were their key challenges and successes, and how did they navigate the uncertainties of starting something new? Explore how they made the leap and what advice they have for someone considering this path.

DO YOU HAVE A BIG IDEA YOU'D LIKE TO EXPLORE?

- If so, what are three concrete actions you can take now—whether it's validating your idea, securing a mentor, or researching the market—to move your idea forward, even while you're in your current role?

REFLECTION

HOW CAN YOU SURROUND YOURSELF WITH OTHERS WHO CAN HELP YOU?

- Who are the key people (mentors, advisors, potential partners) who can provide feedback, support, or encouragement? How can you leverage communities, incubators, or networks to build the foundation for your venture?

- What risks are you willing to take? What aspects of your current situation (career, lifestyle, financial) can you shift to support taking this leap? Reflect on the personal, professional, and financial risks, and consider how you can mitigate them while still taking action.

"We do not learn from experience . . . we learn from reflecting on experience."

–John Dewey (philosopher, educational reformer, psychologist)

Develop a Reflective Practice: Unlock the Power of Your Experiences

We've covered four types of experiences to accelerate your learning. Let's shift to amplifying these opportunities for growth through reflection. While you have been reflecting through this workbook, I'd like to suggest that you develop a reflective practice as part of your work and personal life. Without taking the time to pause, you may miss the valuable insights from your experiences. The simple act of reflecting on what worked, what didn't, and what you've learned is one of the best tools you have to extract the lessons from your experiences.

Make it a habit to think about and review your experiences, knowing reflection deepens the learning.

Reflect with intention: It doesn't have to be complicated

Reflection doesn't have to be a long, drawn-out exercise. In fact, the most profound insights can come from just a few minutes of intentional introspection. Find a quiet space, grab a pen (or open your preferred digital tool), and jot down your thoughts. Write about what's going well, what's been challenging, and even the parts that you're unsure about. Don't worry about perfection–this isn't about grammar or structure. It's about the clarity you gain by reflecting honestly and deeply.

Make reflection a habit: A tool for continuous growth

The key to effective reflection is consistency. I recommend setting up a weekly, monthly, and annual routine that fits seamlessly into your life. For me, Sunday mornings are sacred reflection time–I review the week that passed, take a moment to celebrate wins, and prepare myself mentally for the week ahead. During the week, I also use journaling as a tool whenever I'm feeling stuck or uncertain about how to approach an issue. Reflection helps me reset, gives me clarity, and keeps me moving forward with purpose.

> *"Writing is a process in which we discover what lives in us."*
>
> –**Robert Olen Butler** (an American author and professor)

How to get started: Your journal, your space

- **Pick your journal.** Whether digital or paper, find a space to capture your thoughts. I've found there's something almost magical about writing by hand–it forces you to slow down and truly think. For digital folks, a simple Word document might work, though there are plenty of apps you can try.
- **Make a weekly appointment with yourself.** Set aside 30 minutes each week to reflect. No distractions. Find your ideal time, and protect it like any other important meeting. Some days might work better than others, so experiment and see what fits.

> *"Follow effective action with quiet reflection. From quiet reflection will come even more effective action."*
>
> –**Peter Drucker** ("father of modern management")

WHAT'S YOUR PLAN TO DEVELOP A REFLECTION ROUTINE?

WHAT DEVICE WILL YOU USE? PHYSICAL JOURNAL? A JOURNALING APP?

WHAT TIMEFRAME IS MOST LIKELY TO WORK WITH YOUR SCHEDULE AND LIFE?

Weekly and Quarterly Journal Prompts

Use these prompts as you reflect weekly, monthly, and annually. Pick two or three questions to help you reflect on both your challenges and successes.

Weekly prompts

What were my most challenging moments this week? What were my most successful moments?

What went well? What would I do again, and what might I change next time?

Who were the people involved, and how did they impact the situation?

Were there key people who supported me? Who might have hindered my progress? Do I understand what each of them is trying to achieve?

What skills did I use most effectively? What skills do I need to strengthen?

What self-care practices helped me stay energized and focused?

How well did I maintain my energy and well-being throughout this challenge?

Was I able to maintain a growth mindset? If not, what self-talk might help me stay open and curious?

What are my top three lessons from this week?

Monthly reflection prompts

Reflect on my growth over the past month. What patterns or shifts have I noticed in my leadership? Are there any areas I'm ready to elevate or explore further?

What were my most important lessons?

What were the highlights? Why? What were the factors that contributed to it being a highlight?

What were the lowlights? Why? What were the factors that contributed to it being a lowlight?

Considering my highlights and lowlights, were there any important leadership lessons this month?

Is my job still challenging to me? What changes can I make to gain more capabilities?

Annual reflection prompts

What were my big wins for this year, both personally and professionally?

What were my challenges? How did they shape me?

As I look back, what were my most crucial leadership lessons?

What experiences do I need to keep growing and learning as a leader?

Wrap-Up and Next Steps

Congratulations on completing this chapter! By now, you've learned valuable strategies for leveraging work experiences to fuel your leadership growth. The key takeaway here is that growth happens on the job. You can thrive in challenges and uncomfortable moments by reflecting on both your victories and missteps. The next time you face a difficult situation, remember that it's an opportunity for growth.

In the next chapter, we'll dive deeper into the power of learning from others. You'll discover how surrounding yourself with diverse perspectives and guidance can amplify your leadership development. Keep building on your growth momentum!

CIRCLING BACK TO NANCY'S LESSONS OF EXPERIENCE

Returning to our story of Nancy from page 81, she landed her new leadership role right as the COVID-19 pandemic was beginning. Not only did this bring a fresh set of expectations and challenges, but she also had to navigate an entirely new landscape that no one had ventured into before. Nancy focused on strengthening her learning agility. She surrounded herself (virtually) with those who could help her, paid close attention to the dynamics of the next level, and quickly learned from the mistakes and successes she experienced. She established herself as a transparent leader who was unafraid to speak the truth to power. She also consciously built her resilience by focusing on her health and well-being. For her, that meant morning walks, healthy meals, and getting enough sleep. And I'm happy to report that she continues to thrive, landing higher-level leadership positions and making a profound impact on her company.

“Surround yourself with people who challenge you, teach you, and push you to be your best self.”

–**RICHARD BRANSON** (founder of Virgin Group; adventurous entrepreneur; visionary innovator)

BEING INTENTIAL ABOUT LEARNING FROM OTHERS

Being Intentional About Learning from Others

"Everyone you will ever meet knows something you don't."

–**Bill Nye** (The Science Guy)

In this chapter, we'll explore the last element of the model–the power of learning from others.

1. **Surround yourself with people you can learn from.**
2. **Actively build your network of support.**
   We'll conduct a quick assessment of your current network and guide you through the next steps.
3. **Be very deliberate about what you hope to learn from resources like courses, books, and podcasts.**
   Make a plan to apply any new learnings back on the job.

By the end of the chapter, you will have identified your trusted circle of people and completed an exercise to assess and strengthen your network of support.

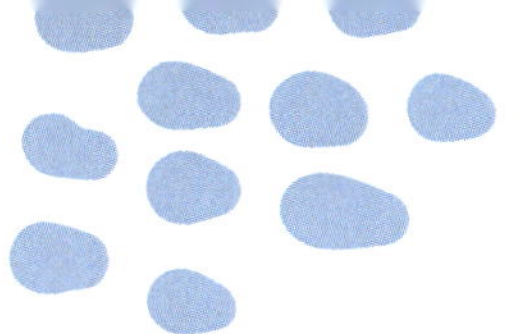

We Don't Develop Alone—It Takes a Village

Another confession. There was a time when I also thought of myself as a self-made person. But as I look back on my journey, I realize there was never a time when my supporters weren't there for me. I may not have seen them as they worked their invisible magic for me, opening doors and connecting me with others, but they were definitely there. I greatly benefited from their kindness and generosity.

It's estimated that ten to twenty percent of our development comes from learning from others. This includes the people who know us well, feel invested in our well-being and success, and want to help us along. They are sometimes very present in our lives; other times, they work behind the scenes for us. We also learn and benefit from people who willingly share their experiences and knowledge through books, videos, blogs, podcasts, and other platforms.

Your support network consists of people who care about your success and can influence your career. This group includes past bosses, current and former mentors and coaches, senior leaders in gatekeeper positions, and colleagues who can connect

BUILDING RELATIONSHIPS IS LEADERSHIP WORK

Susan is a professed self-made woman whose mother raised her from a young age after her alcoholic father abandoned them. She was driven to make something of herself, believing fiercely in her ability to succeed. Susan's grades and achievements earned her a full STEM-based scholarship to a prestigious university. Her hard work continued to serve her at the start of her career. Susan was convinced her work and accomplishments were enough. She found it hard to trust others and maintained the perception that building relationships was a waste of time, so she kept her head down and drove on. Her current and previous boss were the only two people she felt comfortable going to for advice and support. When the tech sector took a dive, Susan was blindsided by a reduction in force (RIF) across the organization. For her, the restructuring resulted in a demotion. Without a strong network of support, she was at a loss to anticipate the changes and navigate the situation. Her two advocates were both swept up in the RIF and were gone. Susan was left to figure out how to move forward on her own.

you to others who might be beneficial. Building your support network is essential for career advancement. For some, this comes naturally, while for others, it's a necessary but challenging task. Regardless, it must happen if you want to enhance your chances of progression and realize your full potential. And, to avoid the situation Susan found herself in in our client story on page 107.

This may be an obvious point, but it is important to keep in mind that the benefit of a large support network includes having access to opportunities that open up through influential people who can advocate on your behalf. It opens doors, connecting you to leaders and opportunities across (and outside) the organization. It also increases the likelihood you'll engage in meaningful conversations about what matters to the organization so that you know how you can better contribute to its overall success. Hopefully, your support network provides feedback when you need it most and is willing to have tough conversations grounded in helping you be a better leader. Ultimately, it helps when times get challenging. Your network can help you navigate through and around sticky situations.

Finding and cultivating supportive people

Imagine yourself surrounded by people who care about you and want to help you grow and succeed. You absolutely deserve this, but it won't happen without effort on your part. Below are several potential relationships that can make a huge difference. Let's identify your circle.

Accountability Partners

Accountability partners are colleagues committed to helping each other grow and learn. Finding a buddy on a similar path, one who is willing to hold you accountable for what you hope to accomplish, provide feedback, and make suggestions. Make sure the relationship is reciprocal by giving as much as you receive. Set up a weekly meeting to review your plans and report on all progress. Share disappointments, triumphs, and stories over a much-needed lunch out of the office.

Who currently serves as your accountability partner(s)? If no one comes to mind, who might be a good candidate(s)? These people are typically our peers.

Believing Mirrors

Julia Cameron (author, artist, creativity coach) describes people who believe in you and see your potential as "believing mirrors." These individuals recognize your uniqueness and are ready to help you see your gifts clearly.[27] When we need encouragement, these are the people to seek out. They can work alongside us, but many believing mirrors are our closest friends and family.

Who are your believing mirrors?

Mentors

Mentors are experienced, trusted advisors. In my experience, most leaders are eager to play this role. They just need to be asked, and they often appreciate the chance to be useful in a different way. The key is to make it easy for them to assist you. Most organizations encourage experienced leaders to nurture the next wave of leadership, so take advantage of this. By making it easy and straightforward for your potential mentors to help, you increase the likelihood of their engagement and support.

If you are fortunate to have a mentor, invest time in nurturing the relationship. This could be through regular meetings, emails updating them on your progress, and staying connected and in touch. Remember, it's not just about what you receive, but also what you give back. There are numerous opportunities for you to reverse the mentor role, and your efforts will be appreciated. Pay attention to your mentor's daily challenges, however small they might be. Maybe you can help refresh their social media. Maybe you can volunteer to review something they are working on. The key is to maintain a healthy, balanced relationship by making it easy, enjoyable, and rewarding for them to engage with you.

Need a mentor? Finding the right person with the needed experience and knowledge can be daunting. Even if you find the right person, they may not have the required time or capacity. So, why not seek mentors for different aspects of your needs? Say you really want help navigating political situations in your department; find the person who's politically savvy. If you are working on developing your strategic agility, find the person who's good at thinking through and creating strategic plans. The point is you may find your "perfect mentor" by piecing together the skills of multiple people and deriving the best of what each has to offer.

Once you identify your mentors, make sure to have a "give back" strategy to balance out the relationships.

Advocates and Allies

Who are the people in your life who will advocate for you when you are *not* in the room? These can be supportive peers or people higher up in the organization with influence or decision-making power. These types of people include your boss' peers and your next-level boss' peers. This group of people may have opportunities opening on their teams. They may also participate in promotion decisions. So, it's important they have a point of view on you and your work.

Here's why. Your work does not speak for itself. It's silent. Completely mute. Only people can speak about you and your work. So, you have to help them by allowing them to get to know you and your contributions.

Who are your advocates and allies? These people typically have the power to influence who gets what job and/or promotion. Don't worry if you are not sure at this point. Look back at Chapter 3, pages 73–75.

Role Models

Find role models you can learn from, whether they are present in your day-to-day life or come in the more abstract form of historical characters or experts you'll never meet. Who are your heroes and heroines? What can you learn from them? In the Reflection section, make a list of your role models. For each person you listed, who influenced their development? What experiences helped shape them as leaders? What strengths did they leverage? What failures and challenges did they overcome?

WHO CURRENTLY SERVES AS YOUR ACCOUNTABILITY PARTNER(S)?

WHO ARE YOUR BELIEVING MIRRORS?

LIST YOUR CURRENT MENTOR(S). WHO AND WHAT SHAPED THEIR LEADERSHIP? HOW ACTIVE IS THE RELATIONSHIP? HOW CAN YOU MAKE THE RELATIONSHIP MORE RECIPROCAL?

WHO DO YOU HOPE WILL BECOME YOUR MENTORS? WHAT DO YOU HAVE TO OFFER THEM? WHAT'S YOUR NEXT STEP?

LIST YOUR ROLE MODELS. WHO INFLUENCED THEIR DEVELOPMENT? WHAT EXPERIENCES HELPED SHAPE THEM AS LEADERS? WHAT STRENGTHS DID THEY LEVERAGE? WHAT FAILURES AND CHALLENGES DID THEY OVERCOME?

Congratulations! You have just listed all types of support people in your circle (except the historical role models, of course). What is your plan to develop and maintain healthy relationships with them?

Your Personal Board of Directors

One way to keep a select group of trusted advisors actively involved in your growth is to invite them to be members of your personal board of directors. Their role is simple: stay curious about your career and life, and offer advice when you need it. This symbolic gesture lets them know you value their insights and active participation. I recommend choosing **five to seven people**—enough to provide diverse perspectives, but small enough to manage and engage with meaningfully.

IF YOU DECIDE TO IMPLEMENT THIS IDEA, WHO WOULD YOU ASK TO BE ON YOUR PERSONAL BOARD OF DIRECTORS? HOW AND WHEN WILL YOU ASK EACH ONE OF THEM?

Your Support Network at Work

Most of us work in companies where other people are the judge and jury of our performance and potential. Knowing how you will be evaluated and by whom is crucial if you want to succeed in the company (a big, complex people system) you find yourself in. Assessing your support network can help you craft a plan to strengthen it.

The exercise below will help you identify:

- The people squarely in your camp who are ready and willing to help you
- The influencers, gatekeepers, or decision makers who can and will influence your career
- Who needs to get to know you better
- What relationships you need to strengthen

PRO TIP: You might complete this exercise with trusted colleagues and/or mentors to get their real time reaction to any assumptions you make or insights you surface. The bottom line is to not do this exercise in a vacuum.

Let's do a quick assessment

1. Using the space on page 115, write down your short-term goal(s). Examples are "Get promoted to VP within the next two years" or "Get a different role in another department."
2. Write your name in the middle of the page.
3. List your peers on both sides of your name. These are the people on your team who don't have decision-making powers but can definitely influence decision-makers. Do they see you as a trusted team member and colleague?
4. If you have direct reports, write their names in the space below your name. Your boss is likely to seek their opinions of you as a manager.
5. Now write your boss's name above your name. They will be the one to nominate you for a promotion or new role. Most companies require some type of justification for a promotion. It usually includes a description of the role and why they think you are ready to step into the role.
6. Write your boss's peers on both sides of your boss's name. These people are very likely to have a say in promotions or assignments at your level.
7. Now write your boss's manager above your boss's name. Write down her or his peers. Depending on your company's procedures, these people are also likely to have a say in promotions or assignments at your level.
8. Can you go another level up?
9. Now, given your short-term goal (e.g., your promotion), who are the people you need to influence and the key decision-makers? Circle each of their names. If you are not sure, work with your manager to understand who the decision-makers are who will influence your short-term goals. This might include someone in the people department or leaders in another organization.
10. Now, assess your relationship with each person. Are they an advocate, neutral, or a skeptic to your goal?
    - **Put a plus sign by your advocates.** Your advocates are those who will support you and support your promotion or other goal.
    - **Put a question mark by those who are neutral.** Your neutral people are those who don't know you and your contributions. They probably will not weigh in on any type of decision regarding you.
    - **And, finally, put a minus sign mark by people who may not view you positively.** These skeptics might argue with your advocates regarding your talents and/or contributions. They may not see you as ready to step into a bigger role or may have had a negative experience with you that has not been resolved.

EXERCISE 10: YOUR SUPPORT NETWORK AT WORK

Short-Term Goal

Your Name Here

Advocate: "+"
Neutral/Unsure: "?"
Skeptic: "-"

REFLECTION

WHAT ARE THE OBVIOUS IMPLICATIONS AND NEXT STEPS?

This usually involves setting up time with people to better understand their challenges and concerns. Get advice from your manager or mentor before proceeding.

Books/Podcast/Coursework/AI

We are lucky to be living in such a knowledge-rich environment where answers to our questions are instantly accessible. Learning new theories, frameworks, facts, and approaches is critical for our growth, but until we apply new knowledge or behavior to our own lives, the full learning cycle won't kick in (remember experience is our greatest teacher). So, as you acquire new knowledge, find a way to apply it. For example, let's say you are reading *this* workbook. What's your plan to implement any ideas that make sense to you?

As we gain expertise, one of the best ways to deepen our learning is to teach it to others or use third-person teaching.[28] If you want to delve deeper into any given topic, record a podcast, teach a class, or volunteer to help others learn what you know.

Leadership development courses

Leadership training courses can be an effective solution if, and only if, key learning points are quickly applied and reinforced back at the workplace. How often have you attended a wonderfully insightful course, but the timing wasn't right for you to immediately apply the learnings to your daily work?

To make your training stick, try these strategies:

- **Set clear objectives before you go.** Ask yourself, *"What do I most want to learn? How will I put it into action immediately?"* Arriving with a purpose ensures your course time is focused and intentional.
- **Block time to practice.** Don't wait until you're swamped. Schedule moments on your calendar before the course to apply what you learn once you return.
- **Create a concrete action list.** During the course, jot down steps you can implement the moment you're back at work. Treat these as commitments, not just ideas.
- **Find an accountability partner.** Whether it's someone who attended the course with you or a colleague who's done it before, share your goals and ask them to check in on your progress.
- **Teach what you learn.** Share your takeaways with your team. Explaining new concepts or strategies aloud not only reinforces your learning but sparks a culture of continuous growth across your team.

Wrap-Up and Next Steps

In this chapter, we covered the last element of the model: learning from others. Hopefully, you have identified your people and assessed your network of support.

In the next chapter, we'll put the four elements of the model together to craft a development plan to help you achieve your short-term goals.

“A goal without a plan is just a wish.”

–ANTOINE DE SAINT-EXUPÉRY
(French writer and aviator)

6

CREATING YOUR HIGH-IMPACT DEVELOPMENT PLAN

Creating Your High-Impact Development Plan

In this chapter, I'll step you through creating your development plan.

1. **Focus on one or two areas to help get you closer to your short-term goals.**
2. **Use your job as the platform for your development plan.**

By the end of this chapter, you'll have a first draft of your plan that you can start implementing immediately.

Creating your development plan is an ongoing, iterative process. And, if you worked through this workbook, you have many of the pieces. Recall that it starts with an inward look at what matters to you–your values and purpose–followed by honest feedback from those around you regarding your strengths and vulnerabilities. With this healthy dose of self-awareness, you articulated your personal and professional goals. You also identified the people who can help you. All this enables you to take advantage of the experiences that will fuel your progress.

Now, let's zero in and consider what actions will get you closer to your short-term goals.

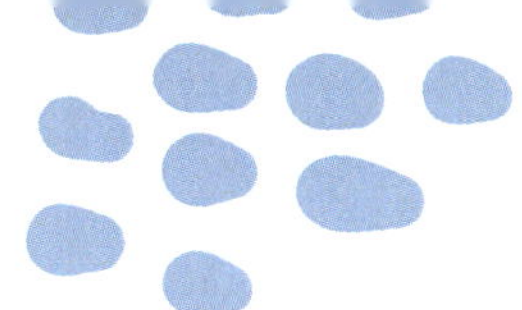

Paths to Growth

As we consider *what* to develop, the tendency is often to focus on our weaknesses. The problem with this approach is that it lacks sustained motivation and impact. Besides, improving your weaknesses may not be the fastest path to achieving your short-term goals. Below are some proven strategies to build a plan that challenges yet inspires you.

- **Clarifying your goals.** Sometimes, the most potent development focus is to declare your intentions or goals. (Remember Vanessa in Chapter 3?) Not only does this help you key in on what you say "Yes!" to (e.g., a job in which you can demonstrate and grow your leadership) and what you give a firm "no" to (e.g., a similar job you've already done) , but it also helps others to know how they can best support you. Opportunities seem to follow clarified intentions. So, if you are still not clear about your goals, double down on clarifying your focus.
- **Is it time for a new role?** If you are not challenged in your current role, one of the most impactful things you can do is to find a new role within your company (if you love the place) or outside if you don't believe you can have a great career at your current employer.
- **Leveraging your signature strengths.** Sometimes, the best way to accelerate your development is to leverage your superpowers more powerfully. Suppose one of your superpowers is having empathy for others. You might put this to use by better understanding your customers to glean competitive insights and better meet their needs. Or say your gift is in financial analysis. How could you demonstrate this strength to solve a vexing problem for the business?
- **Proving yourself in an untested area.** Often, we find ourselves in roles that we've mastered but have not actively demonstrated skills that are needed for the next big career move. The classic example is the transition from individual contributor to managing others. If this resonates with you, talk to your manager about leading an effort that involves directing the work of several people–

practice managing others before you have the official responsibility for it. You'll also be gaining proof that you are ready to lead others.

- **Improving a skill you are only average in.** If your target job is competitive, you may need to differentiate yourself by demonstrating mastery of some skill or competency that may currently be in your "average" category but is a game-changer for the role you hope to snag. For example, let's say you can deliver a decent presentation. You've got your eye on a role that requires inspiring large groups of people. You may choose to enhance your storytelling skills by working with someone masterful at engaging others through storytelling.
- **Building a network of support.** Let's say you have been ready for the next big move for some time. You can demonstrate your experience and results, feel confident that you can excel, but feel frustrated that you do not hear about opportunities for potential roles before they are announced. You hear about new jobs too late and keep missing opportunities, suggesting that you have a network problem (Circle back to Chapter 5). It may be time to focus on building your relationships with those in the know.
- **Preventing derailment due to a vulnerability or overused strength.** There are times when working on your weaknesses becomes imperative, especially if you are struggling in your job and your performance needs improvement. If you are in this situation, it's time to take a hard look at your personal and professional goals. You may not be in a position that will ever feel right and take full advantage of your strengths. Take a big step back and reevaluate. What needs to change?

Let's Get to Work!

Open your completed **What Matters Most** document so that you can cut and paste elements of it into your development plan. Now open and complete the document called **Development Plan for Leaders.**

STEP 1. Going inward: Development from the inside out

Review the following from your What Matters Most document.

- Your key roles
- Values you live by
- Purpose statement

Enter your role, values, and purpose statement in your development plan.

STEP 2. Your strengths and vulnerabilities

Hopefully, the exercises you've completed previously have given you a better view of your strengths and vulnerabilities.

If you are still struggling with identifying your strengths:

- What were some of your highest scores on your 360? Read through the open-ended comments.
- Review any personality assessments you have completed.
- Talk it through with trusted colleagues and family.

Now fill in the strengths and vulnerabilities table in your development plan.

STEP 3. State your goals

Now, copy your short- and long-term professional and personal goals in your development plan. As you review your goals, ask yourself the following questions.

- Are your short-term goals challenging and inspiring to you?
- Do your long-term goals reflect what you to want to accomplish or experience in the next five to seven years?
- Are you playing it safe and not reaching enough?
- What would you do if your fears (and perhaps a fixed mindset) did not exist?
- Do your values and strengths support your goals?

STEP 4. Narrow your focus: Pick one or two areas that move you closer to your short-term goals

This may include tackling a key challenge in your current role that will help you stand out. Choose development objectives in areas relevant to the work and personal life you are currently living, and that are realistic given those scenarios. Focusing on skills too far away from your current role increases the probability you'll be frustrated with your progress. Life's priorities will inevitably get in the way. The idea is to feel forward movement and get small wins early in your current role to keep you motivated and focused.

Try to embed your development objectives within the context of your current role. Remember: Actual experience is where you'll learn seventy percent of your leadership lessons. How can you push yourself out of your comfort zone to where real learning begins?

REFLECTION

WHAT ARE ONE OR TWO AREAS THAT WILL MAKE THE MOST SIGNIFICANT DIFFERENCE IN YOUR SHORT-TERM GOALS?

It's easy to get carried away with the ten things you must accomplish. Focus is key. Once you complete a growth activity and feel you have improved or strengthened your skills, pick the next step to move you closer to your goals.

Here's an example. One of Claire's short goals is to get promoted to an executive level within her company. In discussions with her manager, she realizes she needs to demonstrate her ability to influence others outside her department. This objective makes sense to her, given the role of an executive stretches across functional and team boundaries.

EXERCISE 11: CLAIRE'S EXAMPLE

DEVELOPMENT OBJECTIVE #1	DESCRIBE THE DEVELOPMENT OBJECTIVE	ESTIMATED COMPLETION DATE
Influencing decision makers outside my department.	*Demonstrate I can influence the thinking and decision making of leaders in product development, sales, and marketing.*	*By August 30*

For each focus area, answer the following questions:

- **How will you define success?** How will you know you've accomplished your development goals?
- **Who notices your accomplishments and why?**

EXERCISE 11: CONTINUING WITH CLAIRE'S EXAMPLE

DEVELOPMENT OBJECTIVE #1	DESCRIBE THE DEVELOPMENT OBJECTIVE	ESTIMATED COMPLETION DATE
Influencing decision makers outside my department.	*Demonstrate I can influence the thinking and decision making of leaders in product development, sales, and marketing.*	*By August 30*

WHAT DOES SUCCESS LOOK LIKE?	WHO NOTICES? WHO WILL JUDGE YOUR SUCCESS?
My boss' peers consider my insights and opinions as they make key decisions.	*My boss, my boss' boss*
My customer research influences the next version of our product roadmap and our go-to-market strategies.	*My boss, my boss' boss, Sally Smith, Mike Hammer, John Perry, Michelle Groves*
Leaders reach out to me for my opinion. I'm receiving emails and calls from decision makers outside my department. They ask me to present to their teams.	*I'll keep track of this one, recording each request I receive from decision makers in my development journal.*

EXERCISE 11: YOUR DEVELOPMENT FOCUS

DEVELOPMENT OBJECTIVE #1	DESCRIBE THE DEVELOPMENT OBJECTIVE	ESTIMATED COMPLETION DATE

WHAT DOES SUCCESS LOOK LIKE?	WHO NOTICES? WHO WILL JUDGE YOUR SUCCESS?

Now, what specific, concrete steps do you plan to take? Think about the people you need to connect with as you work. Make sure each action has a due date. Be sure to leverage your strengths.

EXERCISE 12: AN EXAMPLE FROM CLAIRE

WHAT ACTIONS? HOW CAN YOU LEVERAGE YOUR CURRENT WORK SITUATION TO ACHIEVE THIS OBJECTIVE? HOW CAN YOU LEVERAGE YOUR STRENGTHS? *Influencing the roadmap is a big part of my role. Developing trusting relationships with others and listening are two of my strengths.*	BY WHEN?
Set up one-on-one meetings with Sally Smith, Mike Hammer, John Larson, and Michelle Groves to understand their challenges and share research that might help their businesses. Establish regular meetings. Ask if I can share my team's research at their staff meetings.	*February 1*
Record all key product meetings on my schedule, then work to be included on the invitation list.	*February 1*
Spend thirty minutes a week learning from others about influencing. Listen to podcasts, read articles, and watch Ted Talks regarding influencing others. I'll also start using AI to help guide my learning.	*Schedule a recurring morning slot for learning by February 1*
Book bi-weekly meetings with myself to reflect on the progress I'm making in influencing decision makers outside my division.	*By March 15*
Set up time with my peers to exchange ideas. Share my ideas, listen for ways to strengthen them, and commit to helping my peers with their ideas and goals. Set up a recurring meeting for Dave, Tony, Nancy, Steve, and myself.	*By March 15*

EXERCISE 12: YOUR ACTIONS

WHAT ACTIONS? HOW CAN YOU LEVERAGE YOUR CURRENT WORK SITUATION TO ACHIEVE THIS OBJECTIVE? HOW CAN YOU LEVERAGE YOUR STRENGTHS?	BY WHEN?

One Down and One to Go!

What's one more area that, if you learned or demonstrated, would move you closer to your short-term goal? For example, many leaders are asked to demonstrate their ability to think strategically or to build their teams. If you've been in a role for some time and are hoping to get promoted, thing two is almost always a bit of networking.

STEP 5. One well-being goal

Corporate life can be brutal on your physical and emotional health. You'll receive bonus points in the form of well-being for doing even just one thing that helps you be more grounded or centered. It could be as small as parking in the far-back lot to gain a few more steps and have the chance to be mindful about your day ahead. It could be setting a weekly date with your significant other without any devices, or finally taking that yoga class you've been meaning to take. After you fall into a routine with that one thing, you can set your sights on another to add to it. Baby steps build great habits and self-care routines.

STEP 6. Make it happen

It's go time! Start implementing your development plan today, focusing on getting some early wins. Keep a reflection journal, take field notes to draw your attention to your learning, and mark your progress more generally. Do, assess, course correct, then rinse and repeat.

STEP 7. Review and update: Create a development routine

Keep your development plan a dynamic, living, breathing way of life by reviewing and updating it regularly. Schedule a weekly calendar appointment with yourself to check your progress and reflect on your experience. Share all or parts of your plan with your manager so she/he can best support you. Engage a coach or a group of trusted colleagues and friends to help keep you accountable.

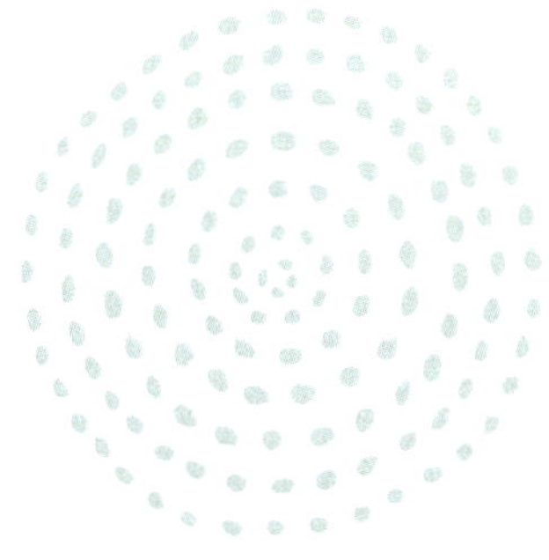

WHAT'S YOUR ONE WELL-BEING GOAL?

WHAT'S THE ONE THING YOU CAN DO RIGHT NOW TO BEGIN IMPLEMENTING YOUR PLAN?

WHAT'S YOUR PLAN TO SHARE IT WITH YOUR MANAGER AND MENTOR? OTHERS?

What to Avoid in Your Development Plan

Now for a bit of a rant on what your development plan should *not* be. It should *not* be a list of courses you must complete or books you will finish. Including articles, books, and coursework in your plan is fine, if and only if you have experiences outlined in your plan to ensure you'll apply what you learn in training to real-life scenarios. Only in this way will those classes and great content help you further your developmental progress. Remember, experience is your best teacher!

Promise yourself all development plans going forward won't solely focus on deficiencies. Promise yourself to identify your strengths and leverage the hell out of them.

Need some inspiration? Use this QR code to check out example development plans.

One last checklist to complete as you review your development plan

- ☐ My personal and professional short-term goals are clear.
- ☐ I have my long-term goals for both my personal and professional life. (Don't worry if you're not sure how to achieve them yet.)
- ☐ Each development objective is clearly defined by how I will measure it and who will judge my progress.
- ☐ My strengths, as well as values, are reflected in my action steps.
- ☐ All my action steps have deadlines.
- ☐ Seventy-five percent or more of my action steps are embedded in my current role.
- ☐ I am developing and/or tapping into my network of support.
- ☐ My plan reflects how I will learn from others.

Wrap-Up and Next Steps

Congratulations! You have your first draft of your dynamic development plan. Remember, this plan is a living document. Once created, it is up to you to keep updating and refreshing it as you achieve your development objectives and career goals. Once you do, revise your short- and long-term goals and start the cycle again and again.

"It is not the strongest of the species that survive, nor the most intelligent, but the one most responsive to change."

–**CHARLES DARWIN** (pioneering naturalist, revolutionary thinker)

7

CONCLUDING THOUGHTS ON MAKING IT HAPPEN

Concluding Thoughts on Making It Happen

Dear Reader,

As we end, I want to remind you of the purpose of this workbook: to empower you to take control of your leadership development, to build your self-awareness, and to cultivate the mindset and tools that will guide you on your leadership journey.

Throughout this workbook, you've worked through exercises that helped you uncover what matters most to you, refine your values, and clarify your goals. You've mapped your leadership narrative, identified your strengths, and embraced your vulnerabilities—gaining insights that will support you as you move forward. You've learned that experience is our greatest teacher, so make sure you are in a role that is challenging you and helping you grow closer to your short- and long-term goals. You have also identified your circle of people who can help support you. Now, the real work begins.

Learning something new and making lasting change is no easy feat. You may experience moments of exhilaration mixed with moments of discomfort, uncertainty, and perhaps frustration. That's all part of the growth process. If it were easy, you wouldn't be evolving into the leader you're meant to be.

As you continue to move forward, keep your mindset focused on growth. Every step, whether small or large, is a step toward your vision. Progress, not perfection is the mantra here. Each lesson you learn, every course correction you make, and every challenge you face will serve as fuel for your continued development. This workbook was designed to help you navigate those twists and turns, and you have already made incredible strides.

What's your next step? The world is waiting for your leadership.

The tools, mindset, and strategies you've explored here are the foundation for the leader you will become. Take charge of your next steps—continue to use the resources and insights you've gathered to fuel your growth.

Remember to bring other leaders along with you on this amazing journey. Keep paying it forward.

"You are your best thing."

–Toni Morrison (writer, winner of Pulitzer Prize for fiction and the Nobel Prize in literature)

One Final Checklist

Before you leave this workbook, here's a reminder of the actions you need to take to keep your leadership development on track.

- ☐ **Clarify what matters most:** Make sure your values and priorities are clear–and keep them front and center as you lead.
- ☐ **Leverage your current role as a learning platform:** Even in roles that feel temporary or routine, there's room to learn and grow.
- ☐ **Build your board of directors:** Surround yourself with people who challenge and support you–mentors, role models, and peers who will help guide you.
- ☐ **Create and update your development plan:** Keep your plan current. Your leadership journey will evolve, and your goals must evolve with it.
- ☐ **Seek feedback regularly:** Growth comes from continual feedback. Don't wait for the next formal review. Get regular input from those you trust and respect.
- ☐ **Build a reflective practice:** Make reflection a part of your ongoing process. Learning from your experiences will continue to sharpen your leadership skills.
- ☐ **Notice your self-talk:** Replace negative talk with compassion and encouragement. Speak to yourself like you would speak to a longtime friend.
- ☐ **Rinse and repeat:** Leadership development is a lifelong journey. Commit to continually revisiting these practices and refining your approach.

You have taken important steps toward mastering the essential skill of developing yourself and others. But remember, this is only the beginning. You now have a clearer sense of who you are, what you want, and how you can make an impact in the world.

My highest hope is that you take on this journey with joy, confidence and clarity. Keep moving forward, trusting in your ability to evolve as a leader, and always remember–you've got this.

Go make a profound difference in this world!

With much love,
Angie

Endnotes

[1] Morgan W. McCall, Michael M. Lombardo, Ann M. Morrison, *Lessons of Experience: How Successful Executives Develop on the Job*, published July 1, 1988.

[2] Michael M. Lombardo and Robert W. Eichinger, *The Leadership Machine: Architecture to Develop Leaders for Any Future*, 3rd ed. (Lominger, 2000).

[3] The Society for Industrial and Organizational Psychology Professional Practice Series, *The Age of Agility: Building Learning Agile Leaders and Organizations* (Oxford, New York: Oxford University Press, 2021).

[4] Shared in interviews and keynote talks on leadership and career development, emphasizing defining success on your own terms (Fast Company, 2012).

[5] The Society for Industrial and Organizational Psychology Professional Practice Series, *The Age of Agility.*

[6] Tasha Eurich, "What Self-Awareness Really Is (and How to Cultivate It)," *Harvard Business Review*, June 2018.

[7] Tasha Eurich, *Insight: Why We're Not as Self-Aware as We Think, and How Seeing Ourselves Clearly Helps Us Succeed at Work and in Life* (Currency, 2017).

[8] Lombardo and Eichinger, *The Leadership Machine.*

[9] Marshall Goldsmith and Mark Reiter, *What Got You Here Won't Get You There: How Successful People Become Even More Successful* (Hachette Books, 2007).

[10] Douglas T. Hall, "The Protean Career: A Quarter-Century Journey," *Journal of Vocational Behavior* 65, no. 1 (August 1, 2004): 1–13, https://doi.org/10.1016/j.jvb.2003.10.006.

[11] Ans De Vos and Nele Soens, "Protean Attitude and Career Success: The Mediating Role of Self-Management," *Journal of Vocational Behavior* 73, no. 3 (December 1, 2008): 449–56, https://doi.org/10.1016/j.jvb.2008.08.007.

[12] Marco S. Direnzo, Jeffrey H. Greenhaus, and Christy H. Weer, "Relationship between Protean Career Orientation and Work–Life Balance: A Resource Perspective," *Journal of Organizational Behavior* 36, no. 4 (2015): 538–60, https://doi.org/10.1002/job.1996.

[13] Eurich, *Insight*.

[14] Eurich, "What Self-Awareness Really Is (and How to Cultivate It)."

[15] Victor J. Strecher, *Life on Purpose: How Living for What Matters Most Changes Everything* (HarperOne, 2016).

[16] Lombardo and Eichinger, *The Leadership Machine.*

[17] Fabio Sala, "Executive Blind Spots: Discrepancies Between Self- and Other-Ratings," *Consulting Psychology Journal: Practice and Research* 55, no. 4 (2003): 222–29, https://doi.org/10.1037/1061-4087.55.4.222.

[18] Carol S. Dweck, *Mindset: The New Psychology of Success, updated edition* (Ballantine Books, 2007).

[19] Dweck, *Mindset.*

[20] Richard M. Ryan and Edward L. Deci, "Self-Determination Theory and the Facilitation of Intrinsic Motivation, Social Development, and Well-Being," *American Psychologist* 55, no. 1 (2000): 68–78, https://doi.org/10.1037/0003-066X.55.1.68.

[21] Howard J. Klein et al., "When Goals Are Known: The Effects of Audience Relative Status on Goal Commitment and Performance," *Journal of Applied Psychology* 105, no. 4 (2020): 372–89, https://doi.org/10.1037/apl0000441.

[22] McCall, Lombardo, and Morrison, *Lessons of Experience.*

[23] The Society for Industrial and Organizational Psychology Professional Practice Series, *The Age of Agility*, Chapter 5.

[24] Kenneth P. De Meuse, "Learning Agility: Its Evolution as a Psychological Construct and Its Empirical Relationship to Leader Success," *Consulting Psychology Journal: Practice and Research* 69, no. 4 (2017): 267–95, https://doi.org/10.1037/cpb0000100.

[25] Eyring, Alison, *Pacing for Growth: Why Intelligent Restraint Drives Long-Term Success* (2017).

[26] Jim Loehr, *The Corporate Athlete Advantage: The Science of Deepening Engagement*, 2008.

[27] Julia Cameron, *The Artist's Way: 25th Anniversary Edition* (n.d.).

[28] Stephen Covey, *The Seven Habits of Highly Effective People* (Free Press, 1989).

About the Author

With more than thirty years of experience in leadership development, Angie McDermott dedicated her career to helping leaders, teams, and organizations unlock their full potential. Whether she's partnering with CEOs or emerging leaders, her mission is to create environments that foster continuous growth, adaptability, and the ability to lead with purpose and impact. That same commitment to transformation is at the heart of this workbook.

After earning her PhD in industrial/organizational psychology from the University of Houston, she began her career at Procter & Gamble, focusing on people research and organizational development. Her journey continued at Dell Technologies in leadership development and later as head of HR for several technology companies, where she helped take two firms to initial public offering and led multiple M&A integrations before founding McDermott Group Consulting.

For the past several years, she has also taught Organizational Behavior to undergraduates and Leading for Impact to executive MBA and TEMBA programs at The University of Texas at Austin's McCombs School of Business. Her teaching brought together applied leadership experiences, such as nonprofit capstone projects, with frameworks for learning agility, resilience, and strengths-based growth.

Outside of work, she is a marathon runner, traveler, and enthusiastic host who loves diving into creative projects. She also loves supporting nonprofit organizations in her community. These experiences have shaped her leadership philosophy, grounded in endurance, curiosity, and the belief that leadership is a continuous journey of learning and transformation.

CONNECT WITH ANGIE:

www.mcdermottgroupconsulting | LinkedIn: @AngieMcDermott

Made in the USA
Coppell, TX
09 February 2026

70550056R10083